Battlegrour
NORMA

CW00550198

CHERBOURG

Battleground Europe
NORMANDY

CHERBOURG

Andrew Rawson

Pen & Sword
MILITARY

First published in Great Britain in 2004 by
Pen & Sword Military
an imprint of
Pen & Sword Books Ltd
47 Church Street
Barnsley
South Yorkshire
S70 2AS

ISBN 1 84415 083 6

A CIP catalogue record for this book is
available from the British Library

Typeset in Palatino

Printed and bound in the United Kingdom by CPI

Pen & Sword Books Ltd incorporates the Imprints of Pen & Sword
Aviation,Pen & Sword Maritime, Pen & Sword Military, Wharncliffe
Local History, Pen and Sword Select, Pen and Sword Military Classics
and Leo Cooper.
For a complete list of Pen & Sword titles, please contact
Pen & Sword Books Limited
47 Church Street, Barnsley, South Yorkshire, S70 2AS, England
E-mail: enquiries@pen-and-sword.co.uk
Website: www.pen-and-sword.co.uk

CONTENTS

Introduction and Acknowledgements 6

Chapter 1 EXPANDING THE BEACHHEAD 9

Chapter 2 SEALING OFF THE COTENTIN PENINSULA 19

Chapter 3 19 JUNE - THE OPENING ATTACK 25

Chapter 4 20 JUNE - THE DRIVE NORTH 39

Chapter 5 21 JUNE - SEALING OFF THE PORT 49

Chapter 6 22 JUNE - THE FIRST ASSAULT 65

Chapter 7 23 JUNE - MAKING INROADS
           INTO THE PERIMETER 89

Chapter 8 24 JUNE - THE NOOSE TIGHTENS 103

Chapter 9 25 JUNE - OVERLOOKING THE PORT 119

Chapter 10 26 & 27 JUNE - CLEARING THE CITY 143

Chapter 11 THE FINAL POCKETS OF RESISTANCE 167

Chapter 12 TOURING CHERBOURG 177

INDEX 190

ACKNOWLEDGEMENTS

When people are asked to recall what they know of about the American involvement in the Normandy campaign during the summer of 1944, most immediately refer to the landing on Omaha beach immortalised in Steven Speilberg's film *Saving Private Ryan*. Others remember the airborne landings around Ste Mere Église referring to the Steven Ambrose's book and the film that followed, *Band of Brothers*. Yet for two weeks in June 1944 America's eyes were focussed the capture of the port of Cherbourg, a vital objective in Eisenhower's plan for the build up of Allied troops on the French coast.

Many visitors to the memorials and cemeteries on the Normandy coast pass through the port, yet few know that the city was the focus of a fierce battle, one in which General 'Lightning' Joe Collins VII Corps' suffered over 7,000 casualties. For six days American troops fought their way through the ring of emplacements and strongpoints surrounding *Festung* Cherbourg while German engineers laid waste to the dock facilities, complying with Hitler's order to deny the port to the Allies. The battle for Cherbourg was an important campaign in the history of the Normandy, but it is one overshadowed by the events that took place before it and in the weeks that followed. Hopefully, this book will redress the balance and visitors to the Cotentin Peninsula will take time to understand why the battle for Cherbourg should not be forgotten.

Several people have assisted me in the preparation of this book, and my studies would have been impossible without their help. All the staff at the US National Archives in Washington DC, made me feel particularly welcome and did what they could to make sure that my visit to the USA was both productive and enjoyable. David Giodarno gave me a useful guided tour through the printed documents and continued to keep an eye on me as my work progressed; his assistance was invaluable. Beth Lipford's guidance as I searched through the archives indexing system meant that I received the material I needed on time. Holly Reed made sure that I obtained the photographs I required in the stills department and Tom McAnear worked hard to locate the maps I wanted from the cartography room. They all made sure I had the documents I needed before my departure date; customer service is uppermost in the minds of the staff at the NARA.

In the UK I would like to thank Roni Wilkinson at Pen and Sword for initially suggesting the idea and drawing together my words and illustrations to produce the book you hold in your hands.

Finally, I would like to dedicate this book to my son Alex who accompanied me on my first visit to Cherbourg. Let us hope that his generation only go abroad for pleasure rather than to fight for the freedom of an occupied country.

The inevitable outcome of the Battle for Cherbourg, captured German troops, led by their officers, march off into captivity.

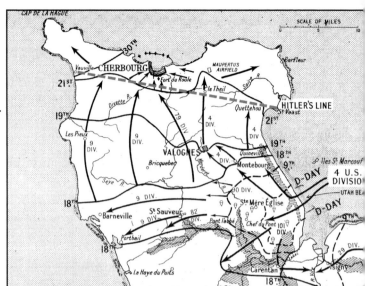

The Cotentin Peninsula; Cherbourg was VII Corps' first objective after establishing its beachhead at Utah. This is how the campaign developed.

Below: the city and port of Cherbourg taken before D-Day

Chapter One

Establishing the Beachhead

Cherbourg had featured heavily in the Allies planning for the landing on the Normandy coast. Once a secure beachhead had been established General Omar Bradley had to secure the port as soon as possible. The build up of troops needed to push inland would quickly outstrip the capacity of the temporary harbours built on the beaches. Planning had been dominated by the need for adequate port facilities to maintain the flow of men, equipment and supplies from England to the front line. VII Corps Field Order Number 1, issued on 28 May 1944 emphasised the importance of Cherbourg:

> *VII Corps assaults Utah Beach on D-Day at H-Hour and captures Cherbourg with minimum delay.*

Meanwhile, V Corps would land on Omaha Beach, securing the area east of the River Vire, linking up with British troops at Bayeux. As soon as the two American Corps had contacted at the town of Carentan, General 'Lightning' Joe Collins, VII Corps commander, could turn his attention to forcing a route across the Cotentin, cutting off Cherbourg from the rest of the German Seventh Army. Originally it had been expected that the port

General 'Lightning' Joe Collins briefs General Eisenhower and General Bradley, First US Army's leader.

VII CORPS

82nd AIRBORNE
The 'All American'

101st AIRBORNE
The 'Screaming Eagles'

4th DIVISION
The 'Ivy Division'

9th DIVISION
'Hitler's Nemesis'

79th DIVISION
The 'Cross of Lorraine'

C47- Skytrains (Dakotas) tow Waco gliders over the Cotentin Peninsula.

would be captured on D+8, but a reassessment of the German troops in the area made a few days before the landings put the date back to D+15.

Following a spell of poor weather at the beginning of June, General Dwight D Eisenhower, Supreme Commander of OPERATION OVERLORD, finally fixed the date for D-Day and during the early hours of 6 June hundreds of bombers, transport planes and gliders flew over the Normandy coast as thousands of men huddled in landing craft and ships headed for the beaches; the Allied assault on Nazi occupied Europe had begun.

The first phase of VII Corps' plan was to land two airborne divisions on the Cotentin Peninsula to secure the inland areas ahead of the sea borne invasion. The paratroopers and glider troops were expected to capture crossings over the Douve and Merderet Rivers but poor weather conditions caused havoc and hundreds of men landed miles from their intended drop zones.

General Matthew Ridgway's 82nd (All American) Airborne Division was either side of the Merderet River. 505th Regiment landed east of the river and secured Ste Mere Église after heavy fighting. Meanwhile, 507th and 508th Regiments were scattered along the banks of the river, where the Germans had flooded the area, and isolated groups of men spent the day fighting for the crossings over the river. Major-General Maxwell D Taylor's, 101st (Screaming Eagles) Airborne Division was also spread over a wide area south and east of Ste Mere Église. Despite the confusion, 501st Regiment pushed south towards Carentan, securing crossings along the Douve River as 505th and 507th Regiments cleared the area inland of Utah Beach.

While the two airborne divisions struggled to secure their

11

Troops come ashore on Utah beach under artillery fire. NARA-111-SC-190109-S

drop zones, the landing craft carrying the first wave of the 4th Infantry Division were approaching Utah Beach. Three out of

Major-General Raymond Barton. Having secured Utah Beach, 4th Division would play an important role in the attack on Cherbourg.

the four craft responsible for guiding the landings were either disabled or sunk at an early stage and the remaining vessel struggled to guide the division ashore in the strong offshore currents. The division landed over a mile south of their intended target where the beach defences were weaker than expected and Major-General Raymond O Barton's men pushed inland quickly having suffered only light casualties. Within a few hours of landing the leading elements of the 4th Infantry Division had met up with paratroopers of the 101st Airborne east of Ste Mere Église. The landings were underway and by nightfall over 20,000 men and 1,700 vehicles had been put ashore on Utah Beach. Hitler's pledge to stop an Allied invasion at the water's edge had failed; the Atlantic Wall had been breached.

Troops continued to pour ashore the following day and although German resistance was weaker than anticipated, progress inland was slow. 101st Division reinforced its hold along the River Douve with the help of one of 4th Division's Regiment's while the rest of Major-General Barton's men attempted to clear the coastal fortifications north of Utah Beach. 82nd Division was again unable to secure a passage across the River Mederet and the setback severely limited consolidation of the beachhead's western tip. General Ridgway's men eventually

Men of the 101st Airborne Division share their rations with the local population. NARA-111-SC-191163

captured the La Fière causeway on 9 June and later that night 90th Infantry Division began to relieve the beleaguered paratroopers with orders to push west of the Merderet.

4th Division was also experiencing difficulties securing the area south of Montebourg, and 9th Infantry Division sent one of its Regiments to assist in clearing the batteries along the coast when it came ashore on 10 June. The following day General Barton was able to report that his men had finally secured its D-Day objectives, the high ground between Le Ham and Quineville.

Once VII Corps had established a solid beachhead, General Collins turned his attention to linking up with V Corps at Carentan. 101st Division's attack across the River Douve on 10 June encountered fierce resistance and for two days the paratroopers edged forward along ditches and hedgerows. American troops finally entered the ruins on 12 June and despite counterattacks by German armour and panzer grenadiers, 101st Airborne made contact with V Corps' on 14 June.

4th Division's landing on Utah Beach and the link up with the 82nd and 101st Airborne Divisions.

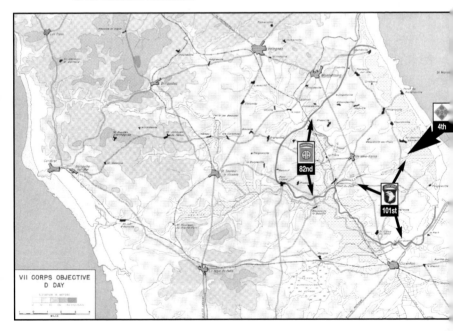

Having liberated Carentan, General Bradley could turn his attention to cutting the Cotentin Peninsula. NARA-111-SC-320862

While progress was being made on VII Corps' flanks, 90th Division had failed to advance far beyond the Merderet River in the centre. Brigadier-General Jay W Mackelvie's men struggled to take their objectives and after four days of repeated failures, General Collins replaced him and two of his two regimental commanders. Mackelvie's replacement, Major-General Eugene M Landrum, realised that his men had to come to terms with the difficulties presented by the Normandy countryside. It was ideal defensive territory covered by a patchwork of small fields, each one bordered by thick hedgerows that severely limited observation and confined vehicles to narrow lanes. Landrum's comments about fighting in this 'bocage' and the merits of the German 88mm anti-tank gun, would apply throughout the battle for Cherbourg and beyond:

> *'Coming under hostile fire causes inertia to our troops, do not believe that they are afraid but bewildered, and this can be broken by common sense, applying simple tactics of fire and movement which are applicable in any type of fighting. It is doubtful whether any man is pinned down unless out in the open... [we]*

Once VII Corps and V Corps had linked up at Carentan, the build up for the offensive on Cherbourg could begin. NARA-111-SC-320865

mustn't let ourselves be stopped by fire, we must get something moving right away. Part of the line may have to take it, but we have to get fire on the hostile weapons, the machine guns. It is seldom that any unit of any size is pinned down, so it should be possible always to manoeuvre some of your forces if there is any concealment at all, and there's plenty of it here... PWs [Prisoners] say they can tell the direction from which we are coming and how we're going, which indicates we've got to control our fire... and they say we bunch up... we should be able to control our men better in this terrain. The danger of the 88 is that it multiplies in quantity as one man tells another about them, and finally our men think there are four times as many as there really are. It is an effective weapon, but it can be beaten, we have plenty of artillery to be used on call.'

9th Division reinforced 90th Division's line west of the river 15 June and the linking up the La Fière and Carentan crossings over the Douve by 82nd Division marked the beginning of a new stage in the campaign. VIII Corps had also begun to take over responsibility for protecting the southern half of First US Army's front; the time had come for General Collins to concentrate on liberating Cherbourg.

US Airborne troops commandeer a German *Kubelwagon*. NARA-111-SC-320864

Chapter Two

Sealing off the Cotentin Peninsula

As soon as 82nd Airborne Division and 9th Infantry Division had secured bridgeheads across the River Douve at St Sauveur-le-Vicomte and Ste Colombe, General Collins was ready to carry out the next phase of expanding the beachhead; a drive across the peninsula. Major-General Manton S Eddy was to send two Regiments across the river, while his third Regiment, the 39th, secured the Corps' right flank around Biniville and Orglandes.

The attack opened on 17 June and 47th Regiment passed through 82nd Airborne's bridgehead at St Sauveur-le-Vicomte, brushing aside small groups of German soldiers as it headed southwest. By nightfall Colonel George W Smythe's leading battalion had reached Grande Huanville, cutting the road between Barneville-sur-Mer and la Haye du Puits and the last escape route from the peninsula.

60th Regiment advanced west from Ste Colombe and pushed quickly through Nehou towards the high ground around St Pierre d'Arth Église. Again there was little resistance and as it began to grow dark Colonel Frederick J de Rohan's men could see the

Major-General Manton Eddy.

coastline ahead as they reached the summits of Hill 145 and 133. German resistance appeared to have collapsed and General Collins was anxious to keep moving throughout the hours of darkness in the hope of reaching the sea before dawn.

General Eddy passed on the message to Colonel Rohan with the words 'we're going all the way tonight' and the plan was for armour to drive Company K into Barneville-sur-Mer while the rest of 3rd Battalion occupied the ridge overlooking the town. At 22:00 five Shermans, four tank-destroyers and four halftracks loaded with infantry headed down to the sea. Although an anti-

Airborne troops pick their way through the ruins of Ste Sauveur-le-Vicomte. NARA-111-SC-190613

tank gun disabled one tank-destroyer en route, German resistance melted away and by first light the armoured column had seized the town, finding only a handful of military police. 9th Division's lightning advance had cut the escape route from the peninsula in record time, leaving thousands of German troops cut of from the rest of Seventh Army.

While 47th Regiment made its advance in to Barneville, columns of German troops tried to break through the American cordon to the east. Infantry surprised 1/39th Regiment's bivouac north of St Jacques de Nehou during the night and as automatic fire ripped through the darkness, Lieutenant-Colonel Tucker's men scrambled to take up their positions. With communications to the rear cut, Tucker ordered his men to retire as the machine guns gave covering fire. One by one his companies broke off contact, keeping the enemy at bay with bayonets and grenades. After several hours, Tucker's radio contact with divisional headquarters was re-established, and as the full weight of available artillery and mortars joined in the battle, the German attack was crushed. When Tucker's men pushed north to the River Seye, they found over 300 dead and wounded scattered around their bivouac area; their own losses totalled forty-five.

An attempt to breach 60th Regiment's lines was completely smashed by artillery fire. 60th Field Artillery Battalion was called up when a column of infantry and artillery units was seen leaving Bricquebec heading for Barneville. Observers directed the guns, walking the barrage up and down the column of vehicles sending men running for cover. The deluge of shells

9th Division's drive to the west coast cut off thousands of German troops on the Cotentin Peninsula.

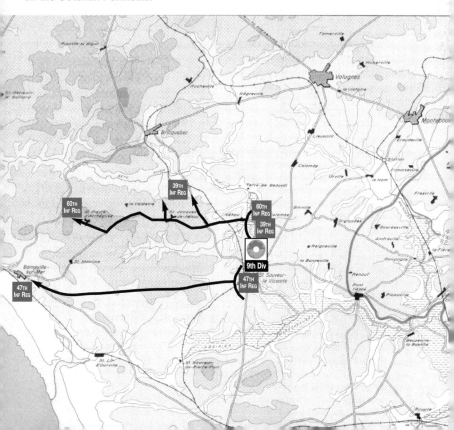

39th Regiment advances through St Jacques de Nehou on their way to the coast.

destroyed dozens of lorries, halftracks, cars, motorcycles and weapons, and completely shattered the breakout attempt. Roadblocks composed of infantry and anti-tank guns dealt with many other small groups of German troops as they tried to break through 60th Regiment's cordon. With the peninsula cut and the corridor secure, General Collins could turn his attentions towards Cherbourg. While 9th Division had driven towards the coast, VIII Corps, under Major-General Troy H Middleton, had taken over responsibility for First Army's southern flank. VII Corps could now concentrate on moving north towards the port.

General Eddy manoeuvred his three regiments into position on the west bank of the River Douve on 18 June while a new formation, Major-General Ira T Wyche's 79th Division, moved into the centre of VII Corps' line, east of the river. 4th Division had

Major-General Ira Wyche.
NARA-111-SC-191299

22

improved its positions on the east side of the peninsula and although shelling and bombing had reduced Montebourg to ruins, Major-General Barton was aware that German troops were preparing to hold the town. Sergeant Duncan, of the 4th Engineer Combat Battalion, took part in one of the patrols sent out to locate German strongpoints for the artillery:

'I went up to about 300 yards from Montebourg and saw the Germans booby trapping all the windows in the houses and blocking the roads and also saw them storing ammunition in a corner building. They were bringing it in little carts and wheelbarrows. I saw an 88 by the bridge on the right side of the road and another on the left. I also saw them setting up two mortars on a little road off to the side. I started firing at the Germans bringing up the ammunition to the corner house. They scattered all over the place. The artillery opened up and they knocked large holes in the church steeple, wiped out the corner building with all the ammunition, knocked out the mortars and

A jeep lies wrecked on a road into Montebourg. NARA-111-SC-190605

also one 88. He said he didn't want to shell the other 88 as there were too many civilians around.'

By nightfall on 18 June, observers reported little movement in Montebourg. It appeared that the Germans had finally moved out to concealed positions either side of the town, where patrols had encountered strong German positions. Estimates put the opposing strength between 1,000 and 1,500 men. Elements of the 2nd Battalion, German 729th Infantry Regiment, and the *Sturm* Battalion AOK 7, had already been identified dug in along the railway line and intelligence reports had reported the presence of the 2nd Battalion, 921st Regiment.

Heavily camouflaged German troops wait for the offensive to begin.

Chapter Three

19 June – The opening attack

9th Division

Major-General Eddy's plan was to advance from Carteret and St Jacques de Nèhou at first light, seizing the high ground six miles to the north. 60th Regiment headed rapidly along the coast towards St Germain le Gaillard while 39th Regiment advanced quickly towards Rauville la Bigot. Meanwhile, four troops of the 4th Cavalry Group operated on the division's right flank, maintaining contact with 79th Division's advance.

As General Eddy's men pushed north, civilians were eager to point out that Germans had already fled during the night and the remnants of the 743rd and 91st Infantry Divisions were

The local population turn out to wave on their liberators on. NARA-111-SC-191016

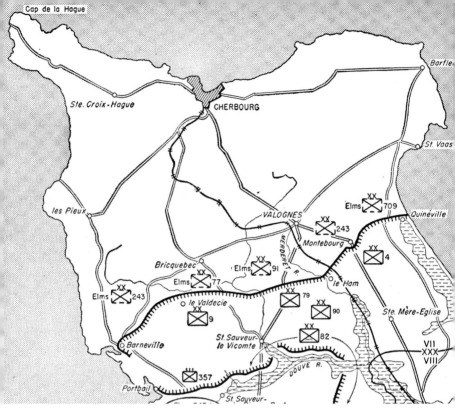

9th Division pushed quickly towards Les Pieux, while the rest of VII Corps encountered strong German resistance.

heading north for Cherbourg. Colonel Rohan and Colonel Smythe's men found that few roads had been mined and many bridges had been left intact a sure sign that the withdrawal had been rapid. 39th Regiment reached Bricquebec on the right flank in less than an hour and quickly established that the Germans had abandoned the town leaving several hundred wounded behind in a field hospital; amongst the wounded were 150 US paratroopers, captured during the early stages the invasion.

Confidence grew as the columns of troops headed north and news of the advance began to spread. In many villages the local population turned out in force to watch the GIs pass by, passing on useful information to their liberators. Several reports of a prisoner of war camp near the village of Le Vretot were quickly followed up and another 400 US Airborne troops were soon released and returned to their units.

39th Regiment's reconnaissance troops made an interesting discovery as they approached the final objective. The body of

Generalmajor Stegmann, commanding officer of the 77th German Infantry Division, was found in a wrecked staff car on the road to Les Pieux. He had been mortally wounded during an attack by an Allied plane as he tried to escape to the south.

By noon both 60th Regiment and 39th Regiment reported that they were on their objectives and the only resistance had been encountered on the division's right flank. Troop A of the 4th Cavalry Group quickly crushed the German position on the outskirts of Rocheville with the assistance of tanks and assault guns. The only other signs of resistance were behind the division's lines as groups of Germans cut off by the rapid advance emerged from their hiding places to attack supply columns. General Eddy ordered Colonel Harry A Flint to move his men into the Babeuf valley and from time to time 39th Regiment was called upon to round up the German stragglers; the largest group numbered over 300.

General Eddy was determined to take advantage of the German withdrawal but his first concern was to establish contact with 79th Division, which had been struggling to keep up on the east bank of the River Douve. While the division regrouped between St Germain le Galliard and Rauville la Bigot, General Collins made a battalion of the 90th Division, the 1/359th Infantry Regiment, available to cover the gap developing between the two divisions.

Motorised patrols scouting ahead failed to establish contact with the retreating Germans and when 9th Division resumed its march north, General Eddy ordered his two Colonels to move fast:

'... keep going until dark and dig in. Keep following enemy up... Make objective right away. Push on. Do everything in the world to maintain communication.'

60th Regiment bypassed the village of Les Pieux and moved quickly along the coast, reaching the high ground around Helleville by nightfall, while 39th Regiment had occupied its objectives, St Christophe du Foc and Couville before midnight. 47th Regiment moved up from reserve and took up positions around Les Pieux, protecting the division's left flank. Yet again, enemy resistance was virtually non-existent and attempts by German rearguards to delay General Eddy's advance were quickly crushed by tanks and tank-destroyers.

9th Division's advance had exceeded all expectations. It had

Medics of the 39th Regiment help a wounded prisoner in Briquebec. The Regiment's motto was 'Anytime, Anyplace, Anywhere, Bar None' symbolised by the marking 'AAAΘ' as seen on the helmet on the right.
NARA-111-SC-190710

covered over eight miles since first light and was closing in on the western outskirts of *Festung* Cherbourg. Overnight, as General Eddy planned his attack, a lieutenant of the French underground contacted his headquarters to pass on useful information about the German positions. Once his platoon of resistance fighters assembled, bringing over forty prisoners with them, the Frenchmen offered to help their liberators, acting as guides and working as interpreters amongst the local population.

79th Division

General Wyche had divided his objectives between the 313th and 315th Infantry Regiments and again the emphasis was on speed. His orders to the Regimental commanders illustrate how the American troops were adapting to their tactics to deal with the difficult terrain conditions:

> 'Mission – *To take high ground north and west of VALOGNES in shortest possible time and to push at least one platoon per company to stream at same time. Prepare to meet counter attack at once, to take high ground by noon... Company COs advised to squirt BARs* [light machineguns] *into corners and to press forward under enemy fire... Engineers to blow new holes in hedgerows and assist. Company of tanks to be ready to be committed on regimental orders.'*

Even though elements of the 77th Infantry Division had been identified opposite 79th Division's front, General Wyche expected little resistance reporting that the enemy was weak for two miles beyond the Line of Departure' and as the GIs moved off, they were prepared for a long advance: 'No rolls, no packs, carry full canteens and D Bars.'

The majority were in action for the first time and wasted ammunition by firing indiscriminately into hedgerows at imaginary snipers and machine gun nests as they advanced along the narrow lanes.

313th Regiment covered four miles in an as many hours, while they maintained contact with 79th Reconnaissance Troop operating along the Douve River. Although civilians reported that German rearguards had stayed behind to slow down the American advance, few were seen as the Regiment approached Bois de la Brique. 1st Battalion sent Company C to investigate Négreville, but rather than finding enemy troops, they met a patrol of the 4th Cavalry who reported that the area was clear. The only signs of enemy activity were two 1,000lb bombs left behind to destroy the bridge across the River Douve.

It seemed as though the Germans were far ahead. However, as 313th Regiment drew close to its final objective, Colonel Stirling A Wood, began to hear reports that his men were coming under fire from the high ground west of La Brique. As firefights broke out all along the line, Colonel Wood called forward a company of tanks to assist his men. 1st Battalion was busy engaging the German troops on their front when trucks crammed with infantry were seen approaching. Lieutenant-Colonel Clair B Mitchell immediately called for assistance and the full weight of his supporting artillery battalion quickly destroyed the column. Despite the heavy resistance, Mitchell

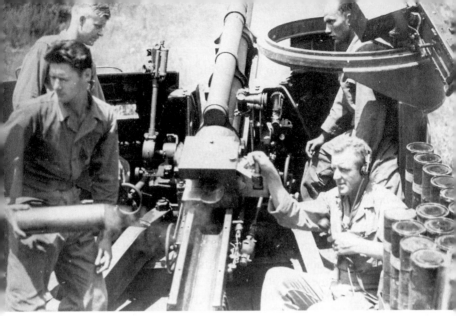

An American Priest, self-propelled gun, provides covering artillery fire.

was able to report to Colonel Wood that his men were 'having one hell of a fine fight!'

3rd Battalion's leading companies were pinned down by strongpoints on the high ground south of La Brique and although armoured support had been requested, the tanks were having difficulty finding the infantry in the maze of hedgerows. Captain Hedges was on his way forward to locate the infantry headquarters when a burst of machine gun fire forced his jeep off the road, sending him diving for cover behind a wall. After radioing for help, two tanks located their leader, backing down several narrow lanes to reach him.

The German machine gun team melted away at the sight of the armour and Hedges was finally able to find 3rd Battalion's headquarters. The infantry directed the two Shermans towards the enemy strongpoint but as the tanks drove forward, anti-tank guns opened fire at point blank range from concealed positions. With no room to manoeuvre, the two tank crews were trapped between the high hedgerows, forcing the tank commanders to fight it out. Shell after shell slammed into the Shermans as the tank crews returned fire and by the time rest of the Captain Hedges' tanks reached the strongpoint, Sergeant Baird's tank had been destroyed after being hit nine times and Sergeant McNeely's had been disabled. They had, however, destroyed the anti-tank guns and the infantry manning the strongpoint had fled. For a second time, the sight of tanks closing in had broken the Germans' will to fight and as darkness fell Colonel Wood's battalions reached the high ground overlooking La Brique village and Bois la Brique.

315th Regiment had a similar experience to their sister Regiment and few Germans were seen during the early stages of the advance. Both 1st and 2nd Battalion came under small arms and mortar fire from a rearguard north of Urville. As Colonel Porter B Wiggins' men prepared to crush the rearguard, the Germans launched an attack from Lieusaint endangering 2nd Battalion's rear and attacking the Regiment's supply vehicles. Neither battalion was in a position to counter the German assault and while Wiggins' 3rd Battalion deployed to deal with the threat, General Wyche was forced to reconsider his plan.

313th Regiment had already reached its objectives but 315th Regiment was heavily engaged southwest of Valognes and still fighting enemy troops behind its lines. To relieve the pressure on his right flank, Wyche ordered Colonel Wood to advance into the Bois de la Brique, reinforcing 315th Regiment. 314th Regiment would move forward to take over 313th Regiment's positions on the division's left flank and push north towards the River Gloire. 314th Regiment had so far spent the day in reserve and some men had struggled to keep out of mischief while they waited and one battalion reported that, 'French women were

A 'remodified' Sherman.

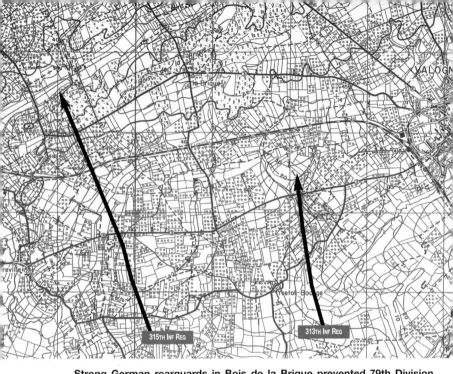

315TH INF REG

313TH INF REG

Strong German rearguards in Bois de la Brique prevented 79th Division cutting the highway north of Valognes.

getting soldiers drunk and asking pertinent questions.' Colonel Warren A Robinson eventually received news of the move late in the afternoon and General Wyche's plan was to transport a

A GI takes advantage of the delay to amuse a youngster.

battalion onto the high ground southwest of Croix Jacobs at the earliest opportunity. Despite the urgency, the change in orders took several hours to organize and by the time the fleet of lorries had found Robinson's 2nd Battalion, it was growing dark. Unknown to General Wyche, *Generalleutnant* von Schlieben, the appointed General of the troops cut off on the Cotentin Peninsula, had already ordered a general withdrawal towards Cherbourg and by the time Lieutenant-Colonel Huff's men dismounted close to their objective, the Germans had already withdrawn.

32

By nightfall 79th Division was holding the majority of its objective. Two Regiments had reached the River Gloire but 313th Regiment had been unable to cut the highway north of Valognes. Although General Wyche had every reason to be pleased that his men had performed well in their first battle, their inexperience meant that several battalions were running low on small arms and mortar ammunition. Throughout the night supply trucks ferried vital supplies to the front line, coming under fire from snipers and machine gun teams cut off by the advance. It would take many hours to round them all up.

4th Division

On the right of VII Corps front, General Barton planned to advance before it was light, hopefully taking the Germans dug in either side of Montebourg by surprise. If possible Barton wanted his men to walk through the German front line before they could react. The divisional artillery had been ordered to hold their fire, only shooting when requested on specific targets to reduce the chance of casualties from 'friendly fire'; regimental mortars would provide the covering barrage. As soon as 8th and 12th Regiments had occupied the high ground northwest of Montebourg, 22nd Infantry Regiment would send a battalion into the town to round up any German troops trapped in the ruins.

8th Regiment attacked the German positions southwest of the town, with the leading platoons hugging the line of bursting mortar shells as they advanced, so close in fact that the high explosive and white phosphorous shells 'burnt their faces'.

Two platoons of 1st Battalion passed right through the German lines, a series of entrenchments along the railway line, and entered Lossiere before they were noticed. The Germans reacted rapidly and the rest of the battalion found themselves pinned down under heavy fire. As it grew light, Lieutenant-Colonel Conrad S Simmons realised that he would not be able to break the German position without armoured support and after recalling the two isolated platoons, pulled back the rest of his men to regroup. 2nd Battalion had more success to begin with and Company F had overrun several enemy positions along the railway, before the Germans began firing blindly into

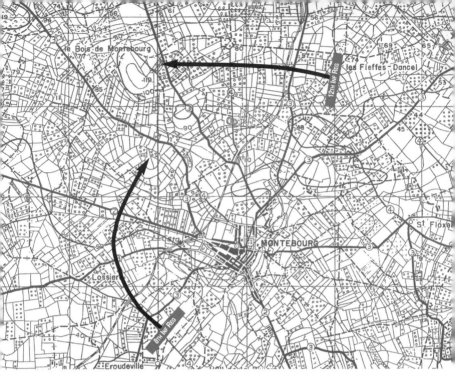

4th Division's initial attack either side of Montebourg failed; the Germans only withdrew when General Barton deployed his armoured support.

the darkness. Lieutenant John A Kulp advanced quickly, expecting the rest of the battalion to follow but by the time he had reached the objective only forty-five men remained; in the words of the After-Action Report, 'the advance was so screwed up that Company F lost two platoons.' The rest of Company F had taken cover in a sunken lane when the Germans opened fire and they were soon joined by Lieutenant John C Rebarchek, Company E's commanding officer. Gathering the men together, Rebarchek led them forward expecting the rest of his company to follow but for a second time the column became lost in the dark.

Lieutenant Rebarchek led the two platoons through the German front line, finding four anti-aircraft guns covering the Montebourg – Valognes highway. After moving close in the darkness, Rebarchek's men charged the position, killing or capturing the crews, before moving on towards the battalion objective. Although Kulp was pleased to see Rebarchek, both officers wondered where the rest of their men were. Until now, neither had realised that they were cut off from the rest of the battalion. Unable to raise their headquarters, the two decided to dig in and wait. As it began to grow light the four platoons scraped out foxholes and looked anxiously to the south for their comrades.

The rest of his battalion was pinned down close to the railway line and when Lieutenant-Colonel Carlton O MacNeely heard the news he went forward only to discover that two of his company commanders were cut off behind the German lines. The Germans were holding slit trenches dug deep into the embankments of a sunken lane and, so far, Company E's attempts to reach them had been stopped by heavy machine gun fire. In many places the German entrenchments were so close to 2nd Battalion's lines that the 60mm mortars were unable to target them. In MacNeely's words, 'the Germans were dug in so deep that they couldn't dig them out'. For a second time that morning Colonel James A Van Fleet heard one of his battalion commanders calling for armoured support.

12th Regiment encountered similar difficulties as it tried to advance through the German lines east of Montebourg aiming to reach Hill 110 and 119 before first light. 1st and 3rd Battalion ran into determined opposition along the railway. Two platoons of 1st Battalion entered the woods on the far side of the railway line before the Germans realised they were being attacked. Elsewhere the response was rapid and deadly. Mortars shelled predetermined points while machine guns put down a murderous crossfire, pinning down the two battalions. Lieutenant-Colonel Charles L Jackson was forced to recall his two platoons from their forward position and as the GIs withdrew to their Line of Departure to regroup, both of Colonel James S Luckett's battalion commanders requested armour to break the deadlock.

As it began to grow light, the confusing situation along 4th Division's front became clear: only two platoons had penetrated the German lines and they were they now cut off to the west of Montebourg. Along the rest of the division's front, companies were regrouping but in places groups of men were too close to the enemy positions to withdraw. All four battalions in the front line needed armoured support to stand a chance of dislodging the Germans from their positions. The dilemma facing the two regimental commanders was how would they deploy their limited reserve of tanks?

GIs escort civilians out of the battle zone. NARA-111-SC-190824

After consultation with the commander of Company B, 70th Tank Battalion, Colonel Van Fleet sent one platoon of tanks to 1st Battalion's assistance and the sight of Sherman tanks moving into position was enough to break the Germans will to fight. Within the hour Lieutenant-Colonel Simmons was able to report that resistance had ended on his front. A second platoon was sent through the outskirts of Montebourg, outflanking the German positions in front of the 2nd Battalion. As the Shermans drew into position, Lieutenant-Colonel MacNeely ordered his men to advance, driving the Germans back and into the path of his two isolated platoons:

'When Lieutenant Kulp and Lieutenant Rebarchek first saw the Germans approaching them from the rear they thought they were being counterattacked. They had already established an all round defence and his company shot down a large number of the fleeing enemy. Some of them were shot in the back as they moved backwards facing the pursuing troops.'

The two platoons of tanks had broken the main line of resistance and by nightfall all three of Colonel Van Fleet's battalions were in position on the high ground between La Victoire and Huberville, to the northwest of Montebourg.

Meanwhile, Lieutenant-Colonel Luckett decided to use different tactics, placing the full weight of Company A, 70th Tank Battalion, behind his 1st Battalion to break the deadlock. Lieutenant-Colonel Jackson ordered his men to advance as soon as the Shermans were in position and once again the German infantry began to withdraw as the tanks approached. This time the withdrawal was orderly and Jackson's men found themselves targeted by mortars and their enemy made skilful use of the hedgerows to try and isolate the Shermans from the infantry. Although the Germans had no armour of their own, *Panzerfaust* teams continually harried the advance as they tried to close in on the tanks.

Eventually, 1st Battalion secured the crest of Hill 110 where the GIs found to their cost that the hill drew fire from every artillery piece and Nebelwerfers in the area. Meanwhile, the company of Shermans headed back to break the deadlock on the right of 12th Regiment's front. 3rd Battalion renewed their attack across the railway line once the tanks were in position and for the second time that day Company A's Shermans advanced slowly through the narrow lanes while Lieutenant-Colonel Dulin's men kept the German infantry at bay.

It was late afternoon by the time 3rd Battalion reached Hill 119, the second of 12th Regiment's objectives. Even so, Colonel Luckett decided to push on to deny the Germans the chance of holding the high ground to his front. 2nd Battalion moved up from reserve and met little resistance as it cleared the summit of the hill (a second Hill 119) and, sensing that the Germans had withdrawn, Luckett decided to keep advancing. The gamble paid off and by nightfall 12th Regiment had occupied Anneville.

The initial resistance on 4th Division's front had delayed General Barton's plan to occupy Montebourg and 22nd Regiment's 3rd Battalion moved into the town several hours later than expected. As the GIs made their way through the ruins initial concerns that German soldiers could be hiding came to nothing. A thorough search only produced thirty prisoners, some dressed in civilian clothes hoping to pass themselves off as locals. Despite the devastation wrought by days of shelling many of the local population had stayed behind:

> 'About 300 of the civilian population emerged from cellars after the Americans entered although the town had been under heavy shelling for more than a week and was completely burned out.'

Once Montebourg had been cleared, 22nd Regiment moved forward onto the Quineville Ridge, extending the division's right flank and established contact with the 24th Cavalry Squadron on the coast. The unexpected German withdrawal during the afternoon had allowed 4th Division to advance far beyond its original objectives and by midnight all three of General Barton's Regiment's were ready to renew the advance at first light.

US troops begin to move through the ruins of Montebourg. NARA-111-SC-191020

CHAPTER FOUR

20 June – The drive north

9th Division

9th Division began to move at first light with 60th Regiment leading. Colonel Rohan advanced north along the coast, looking to trap German troops assembling in the Cap de la Hague area. Again there was little to stop the advance and by midday 60th Regiment had reached the high ground south of Binville and 2nd Battalion began climbing onto the next ridge, Hill 170, ahead of schedule. Unexpectedly, a message from divisional headquarters threw Colonel Rohan's plans into disarray: General Eddy had arranged for the Air Force to bomb Hill 170. Lieutenant-Colonel Kauffman's men were in danger of reaching the target zone too early; 2nd Battalion would have to wait and use yellow smoke when the aircraft approached to indicate

An M7 Priest 105mm self-propelled howitzer heads north.
NARA-111-SC-190413-S

friendly troops. The frustration displayed in Colonel Rohan's message is evident:

> *'White* [2nd Battalion] *wants to know what is going on. Pulled back and men now disorganised. Wants to know why he moved back and what shall we do? Will reorganise and sit tight.'*

60th Regiment's position was far from ideal and 2nd Battalion came under fire from enemy artillery on the high ground to the north. Hedgerows were few and far between on the coastline and Rohan's men cursed the delay as they dug in and waited for the air strikes to begin.

47th Regiment had followed behind 60th Regiment's right flank along the coast, turning northeast at the Bois de Néretz towards Hill 171 and Bois du Mont du Roc, the huge wood covering the summit. General Eddy wanted Colonel Smythe to advance quickly up the hill, and he had arranged for Corps Artillery to shell the Regiment's objectives. So far aerial reconnaissance had not seen any signs of activity on the lower slopes of Hill 171 and 47th Regiment was expected to advance quickly to the Houelbecq stream before it deployed. It was an ambitious plan based on the assumption that the Germans had withdrawn to the summit of the hill and General Eddy was hoping that his men could break the position before the enemy had organised their defence.

In fact the Germans had built a series of camouflaged

Hidden positions on the slopes of Hill 171 brought the advance to an abrupt halt.

outposts on the forward slopes of Hill 171 and 2nd Battalion came under fire from Crossroads 114 as it bypassed Acqueville to the south. The gunfire sounded the alarm and before long both of Smythe's battalions were under 'severe artillery, mortar and small arms fire' as they moved towards the Houelbecq stream.

The strength of the German position had taken General Eddy by surprise and while his headquarters tried to reorganise the artillery support to shell the German outpost line, the two battalions struggled to deploy. 2nd Battalion was pinned down astride the road in front of Crossroads 114 and the GIs sought cover in the hedgerows and ditches. An 88mm shell struck the battalion command post killing both the battalion commander and the artillery liaison officer, also wounding Company F's commander and a number of radiomen and runners. Meanwhile, strongpoints on the far side of the Houelbecq stream blocked any chance of outflanking Crossroads 114.

Colonel Smythe was forced to concede defeat and as his men withdrew to a safe distance, General Eddy considered the implications of the setback. He had originally wanted 39th Regiment to secure the division's right flank, until 79th Division had moved up. It would have then joined 47th Regiment in the centre of the division's line, ready to assault Flottemanville-Hague position. However, the discovery of the German outpost line had seriously disrupted 9th Division's plan and as long as 47th Regiment remained pinned down, 39th Regiment could not deploy.

Meanwhile, 60th Regiment waited in vain for the Air Force to show up and when the advance finally resumed, Colonel Rohan's men encountered strong German positions covering Ste Croix Hague. During the evening, General Eddy instructed Colonel Rohan to prepare to join the rest of the division, leaving one battalion to cover Cap de la Hague. Colonel Rohan was concerned by the change in orders and as German attacks against his flank increased, he called for support:

> 'The situation will leave nothing to my rear. I'll do the best with what I've got. General says keep pushing.'

General Eddy had no other reserves in the area; the rest of the division was either engaged or too far away to assist. The right flank of 9th Division had already come up against *Festung* Cherbourg. There would be no more rapid advances.

79th Division

General Wyche was anxious to clear Bois de la Brique at first light so that the right flank of his division could join the advance. German resistance in the woods had, so far, prevented 79th Division from reaching the Cherbourg highway northwest of Valognes and once the road had been cut 313th Regiment could begin to push north alongside 4th Division. 314th Regiment's objective was Hardinvast to the northwest and while the rest of the division followed the German withdrawal north, 315th Regiment would stay behind to cover Valognes until 4th Division had cleared the ruins.

313th Regiment led the advance into La Brique village and found that the Germans had destroyed the bridge over the Gloire stream. The infantry waded across, leaving behind a queue of tanks and support vehicles and as engineers set to work on a new crossing, using bulldozers to clear the banks of the stream to make a ford, Colonel Wood's men pushed on alone. Fortunately, the Germans had withdrawn the previous night and, after reaching St Joseph, 2nd Battalion headed north

The local population looks on as tanks and infantry head north for Cherbourg. NARA-111-SC-191012

along the Cherbourg highway, finding four abandoned German light tanks and a 88mm gun at Hau du Long.

The Germans had demolished a culvert just beyond the village, blocking the main highway, and for a second time the infantry had to leave their vehicles behind as they waded across. The steep sides of the stream made it impossible to create a ford and as Colonel Robinson's men headed north the engineers started work on two temporary bridges; one for the infantry's support weapons and the second capable of carrying tanks. As the bulldozers set about cutting approach ramps into the stream banks, Lieutenant-Colonel Mitchell, 1st Battalion's commanding officer, arrived on the scene with a truckload of timber 'acquired' in La Brique. The German front line was not far away and Mitchell wanted his men to have armoured support as soon as possible.

The first signs of the enemy were encountered near Samson. Long range machine gun and artillery fire forced 2nd Battalion to deploy into the fields either side of the road. The advance had slowed to a crawl and, as the hours passed, Colonel Wood began to wonder where the Germans would make their stand. The answer came during the early afternoon. As 2nd Battalion approached Delasse, five miles from their Line of Departure, the Germans revealed their positions:

> '... the entire column was brought under fire by 88mm laying directly down the road. The entire forward group lay in the ditches for approximately one and one half hours sheltering from continuous shelling of the road.'

The 88s had turned the road into a death trap and while the men at the head of the column scraped out foxholes under hedgerows, the rest of the Regiment fanned out into the fields to try and locate the enemy positions.

While Colonel Wood's men crept along the hedgerows looking for the 88s around Delasse, the tanks faced a series of frustrating delays. After completing the bridge at Hau du Long, the engineers had to clear a series of craters blocking the road with their bulldozers and by the time the Shermans reached 313th Regiment, daylight was fading. The infantry had failed to locate the 88mm gun positions, leaving Colonel Wood no options; he would have to wait until first light before he could use his tanks.

On 79th Division's left flank, 314th Regiment had deployed

on the north bank of the Gloire stream, extending the division's front west to the Douve River. All three of Colonel Robinson's battalions headed northwest. The Germans had withdrawn, destroying bridges as they fell back, and yet again the advance was delayed as the engineers built temporary crossings over the many streams which criss-crossed the lanes leading to Hardinvast and Tollevast.

After passing through Croix Jacobs 2nd Battalion came across four American paratroopers of the 101st Airborne Division. Their planes had dropped them fifteen miles from the intended target during the early hours of 6 June and for the past two weeks they had hidden in the woods. The paratroopers reported that German units had been heading north for the past twenty-four hours, confirming that the area ahead was clear of enemy troops. Meanwhile, 3rd Battalion found stacks of abandoned equipment near Brix, eight 88mm and two 40mm anti-aircraft guns had also been left behind. The battalion also discovered a V1 rocket complex, (referred to by the American troops as a 'Buzz Bomb' or 'Crossbow' site), comprising bunkers, shelters and concrete launch ramps in the woods south of the village.

American troops inspect a V1 launch site. NARA-111-SC-191169

An anti-tank gun crew set up a roadblock near a wrecked German tank-destroyer. NARA-111-SC-190610

Throughout the spring of 1944 German engineers had built a number of rocket installations on the Cotentin Peninsula and as the Allies prepared to invade Normandy V1 'flying bombs', one of Hitler's terror weapons, began to target the south coast of England. After reporting the news of to divisional headquarters Colonel Robinson ordered his men to push on.

British Commandos of 30 Assault Unit Royal Marines, a unit specialised in collecting intelligence, came forward to investigate the camouflaged installation. A detailed survey, led by an RAF Intelligence officer, Flight Lieutenant David Nutting, followed and within hours the results were being flown back to Allied Bomber Command headquarters in England. For the first time aerial observers had first hand information on the layout of a V1 site and they could use the information to pinpoint similar sites across France and the Low Countries.

1st Battalion came across, what they assumed to be, four abandoned tanks as it approached Haumeau du Long, but as Company A went forward to investigate, the panzer crewmen emerged from their billets. Upon seeing the Americans they began running towards their Panzer IVs. However, a burst of automatic fire served to convince the Germans to surrender and they were quickly rounded up.

All three of Colonel Robinson's battalion commanders reported an increase in German activity as they approached Hardinvast and Tollevast and as daylight began to fail, General Wyche ordered 314th Regiment to halt. He was anxious to avoid repeating 313th Regiment's experience and while patrols probed the German positions, roadblocks were established to guard against counterattacks. Careful reconnaissance was needed before the advance towards Cherbourg continued.

4th Division

General Barton knew nothing of the German withdrawal towards Cherbourg and planned to advance towards Bois du Coudray and Tamerville at first light with all three of his regiments. 12th Regiment quickly established that the enemy had fled, abandoning the high ground north of Saussemesnil and moved into reserve as the rest of the division pushed north. 8th Regiment also found that the Germans had abandoned their

The burnt out ruins of Valognes church. NARA-111-SC-190751

As soon as the German withdrawal had been confirmed, VII Corps took to the roads. NARA-111-SC-191443

positions and once the rest of the Regiment had cleared the area north of Valognes, 1st Battalion sent two patrols into the ruins to search for enemy troops. Although the patrols reported that the Germans had fled, the Allied bombardment had completely destroyed Valognes, blocking many of the roads with huge piles of rubble. It would take several days to clear a way through the debris and in the meantime, VII Corps' supply lines would have to rely on the side roads bypassing the town.

General Barton was concerned that his division was falling behind the rest of VII Corps as it pushed north into the void left by the German withdrawal and ordered Colonels Van Fleet and Tribolet to take to the roads. Reports that General Eddy was already engaging the German fortifications west of Cherbourg were starting to spread and some thought that their own General wanted to reach the port first.

'Rumour has it that the 9th [Division] is within artillery range of Cherbourg. I guess Division Commander Barton is

worried that somebody will beat the 4th to Cherbourg.'

8th Regiment's only encounter with the enemy occurred north of Saussemesnil. Machine gun fire raked a patrol of the Reconnaissance platoon as it drove past a farm, wrecking a jeep. The surviving officer ran back to warn 2nd Battalion about the danger ahead and once Lieutenant Dooley had deployed his men into the fields they worked their way behind the farmhouse. As Dooley's men fired their weapons and threw grenades through the windows, a tank crept forward along the road firing shells into the farm buildings and setting fire to the barn. Eventually, three Germans crawled from the ruins with their hands up and although there was no sign of the machine gun, there was no time to carry out a thorough search. Dooley could see the rest of the battalion backed up along the road but as he ordered his men to resume advance, the owner of the farm came forward:

> *'A Frenchman, very excited, tried to tell them something, but Dooley thought he was just upset about the burning of his barn.*
>
> *Later he heard that twenty Germans were in the burning barn.'*

3rd Battalion's first encounter with the enemy was a line of outposts covering the crossroads south of Ruffosses and in spite of heavy artillery fire, Lieutenant-Colonel Strickland's companies were able to deploy into the fields and press home their attack. 2nd Battalion advanced alongside and the two battalions had cleared the village and the woods to the north before nightfall.

General Barton had been unable to keep in contact with his regiments for long periods as they advanced but by nightfall he was pleased to hear that his men had advanced over eight miles during the day. 22nd Regiment was close to Le Thiel on the right of the division and although his 8th Regiment had failed to reach Hill 178, it was ready to renew the attack at first light. General Barton was also pleased to hear that Bois du Rondou, a large wood in the centre of the division's sector, appeared to have been abandoned by the enemy. Although the division had only encountered the German outposts, as 20 June came to a close, General Barton was poised to attack the main belt of fortifications southeast of Cherbourg.

CHAPTER FIVE

21 June – Sealing off the port

The German Plan

While VII Corps advanced into the void left by the German retreat, General von Schlieben was reorganising his troops to defend the inland approach to Cherbourg. Although the Atlantic Wall was designed to repel an invasion from the sea, Hitler had given orders to protect the ports along the coast of France and the Low Countries from an inland attack. Over the preceding four years Organisation Todt had covered the ring of hills surrounding the port with a belt of pillboxes, entrenchments and wire. Anti-tank ditches and steep sided streams, designed to funnel the American troops towards minefields, both real and dummy, restricted the way forward for tanks. Concealed artillery pieces and mortars supported the German infantry while anti-tank guns covered the narrow lanes. Anti-aircraft batteries, comprising 88mm, 40mm and 20mm flak guns, had been positioned on the hills overlooking Cherbourg and they were all capable of being used in a ground role.

Rolling hills provided the German engineers with an ideal basis for their defensive perimeter and large parts of the Cotentin Peninsula were covered with small fields, each one surrounded by high embankments topped by thick hedgerows:

> 'Perhaps the most striking feature of the terrain was the hedgerows; those countless, centuries old mounds of earth, stone and underbrush bordering cultivated fields, orchards and roads, which were utilised with desperate ingenuity by the veteran enemy troops.'

The local name for the patchwork of hedgerows was *bocage*, a name later associated with the intense fighting throughout Normandy. In many areas the attacking troops would have to thread their way through a maze of narrow lanes and thick hedgerows, while the troops protecting the port watched their every move from their camouflaged positions.

The German troops found a ready-made defensive system as they neared Cherbourg and Lee McCardell, war correspondent for the *Baltimore Sun*, inspected one of the German positions after it had been captured. His report gives an insight into the ingenuity of the German engineers:

'The so called pillboxes in the first line of German defences which the 79th Division assaulted in the attack on Cherbourg were actually inland forts with steel and reinforced concrete walls four or five feet thick. Built into the hills of Normandy so their parapets were level with the surrounding ground, the forts were heavily armed with mortars, machine guns and 88mm guns – this last, the Germans' most formidable piece of artillery. Around the forts lay a pattern of smaller defences, pillboxes, redoubts, rifle pits, sunken well-like mortar emplacements permitting 360 degree traverse, observation posts and other works enabling the defenders to deliver deadly crossfire from all directions. Approaches were further protected by minefields, barbed wire and anti-tank ditches at least twenty feet wide at the top and twenty feet deep. Each strongpoint was connected to the other and all were linked with the mother fort by a system of deep, camouflaged trenches and underground tunnels. The forts and pillboxes were fitted with periscopes; telephones tied in all defences. Entrance to these forts is from the rear, below ground level, through double doors of steel armour plate which defending garrisons clamped shut behind them. The forts were electrically lighted and automatically ventilated. Below a casemated gallery in which the guns were located firing through narrow slits, were two underground bomb proof levels packed almost solidly with cases of canned food, artillery shells and belted ammunition for machine guns.'

General von Schlieben had deployed his commanders in sectors they were already familiar with and *Kampfgruppen* Mueller, formed from the remnants of 243rd Division, held the high ground west of Cherbourg. *Oberstleutnant* Franz Mueller's men had watched closely from Hill 171 and Flottemanville-Hague as 9th Division stumbled on the line of outposts covering the Houelbecq stream. *Oberstleutnant* Guenther Keil, with 919th Regiment and the 17th Machine Gun Battalion, manned a series of entrenchments and pillboxes covering Bois du Mont du Roc and the Divette valley. Further to the east, *Kampfgruppen* Koehn, formed around the remnants of 739th Regiment, held the hills either side of the Trobecque stream in front of 79th Division and the left flank of 4th Division. Meanwhile, 729th Regiment held the fortifications to the east of Cherbourg covering Bois du

An aerial view of a German gun casemate; trenches and dugouts surround the position. NARA-111-SC-191499

Coudray and Maupertus Airfield. *Oberst* Helmuth Rohrbach's command had been severely mauled as it disengaged from 4th Division around Montebourg and many of the battalions had already been reduced to fewer than 200 men.

As VII Corps drew near to Cherbourg, General von Schlieben had given orders to arm every available man in the port to bolster the *Kampfgruppen* on hills around the city. As General Collins' men prepared to attack the German positions, air force personnel, headquarters staff, naval personnel and miscellaneous rear echelon troops joined the German infantry as they waited for the assault to begin. However, while von Schlieben had reinforced the Cherbourg Landfront, he advised Seventh Army headquarters that the morale of some of his

US soldiers inspect a French Renault tank that had been commandeered by the Germans.
NARA-111-SC-190743

troops was suspect, and and noted that,

> *'Good treatment of prisoners on the part of the enemy is very dangerous.'*

As VII Corps drew close to *Festung* Cherbourg it would become apparent that hardened fanatics held some strongpoints, meanwhile, some German soldiers and men recruited from conquered territories were willing to surrender at the first opportunity. It was a volatile mixture, one that would cause problems for both sides in the battle for the port.

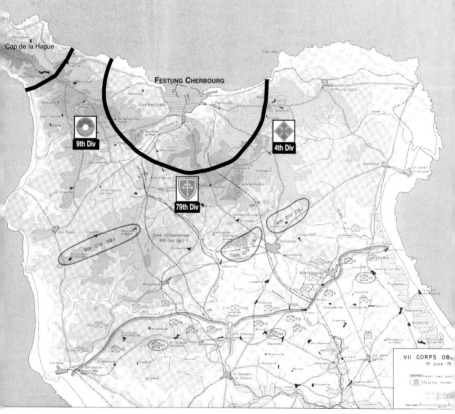

On 21 June American patrols reported a strong belt of fortifications surrounding Cherbourg.

Civilians make their way past a German *Wespe* self-propelled gun as they flee the fighting. NARA-111-SC-190510-S

9th Division

Having established that *Kampfgruppen* Keil's outpost line was along the forward slopes of Hill 171, General Eddy was forced to alter his plans. 39th Regiment would take over 4th Cavalry's position on the right flank of the division, contacting 79th Division across the Divette stream. 4th Cavalry would then move across to the left flank to relieve 60th Regiment in front of Ste Croix-Hague. The previous day's encounter had proved that *Kampfgruppen* Mueller was too strong for a single Regiment and General Eddy intended to screen the Cap de la Hague peninsula while his division concentrated on attacking Cherbourg.

On 60th Regiment's front, Colonel Rohan was determined to clear the enemy positions around Ste Croix-Hague before handing over the area to the 4th Cavalry, but as 1st Battalion patrolled Hill 170, 88mm anti-tank weapons started targeting the battalion area. 2nd Battalion came under heavy fire as it advanced onto the high ground south of Ste Croix-Hague:

53

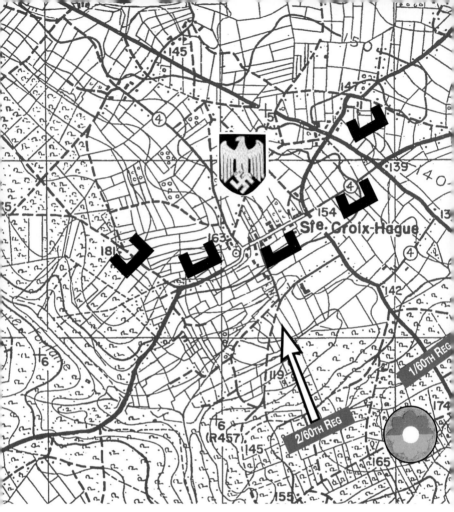

60th Regiment failed to break the German line covering Ste Croix-Hague

> 'Artillery set fire to one tank and shrapnel another. Camouflage net set on fire. It's OK. Germans have zeroed in on us and we can't move. Are going to patrol and try and find trail up at night. Can't advance during the day.'

Lieutenant-Colonel Kauffman's request for assistance was refused; already 3rd Battalion had become heavily engaged as it probed *Kampfgruppen* Keil's line west of Flottemanville-Hague,

> 'Having a hot time here now. Have a new gun on us and don't know where it is coming from.'

2nd Battalion had to push towards Ste Croix-Hague alone but as it tried to infiltrate a wood covering the village a hidden strongpoint opened fire. For a second time Lieutenant-Colonel

Kauffman was in difficulty:

'None of our patrols can get in; I get wounded men on every try. Enemy one hedgerow in front of me; can't send patrols through will have to find a hole in the side to get through. This is definitely an enemy strongpoint. Will lose a lot of lives if I try to bust through an enemy strongpoint here.'

With no reserves to envelop the position, Colonel Rohan ordered Kauffman to withdraw and later that evening 4th Cavalry took over the line in front of Ste Croix-Hague. It would be over a week before VII Corps could to turn its attentions towards Cap de la Hague.

On 9th Division's right flank, 39th Regiment had manoeuvred into position by noon and as it advanced towards Valtot civilians and prisoners freely gave information about the enemy positions ahead. Colonel Flint was hoping to find 4th Cavalry holding Le Ferrange, but as 2nd Battalion advanced they found that the Germans had destroyed the only bridge crossing a railway cutting; it meant that 39th Regiment would have to advance without armoured support.

2nd Battalion crossed the railway only to find that the Germans were waiting on the far side and while machine guns and *Nebelwerfers* targeted Lieutenant-Colonel Gunn's men, Colonel Flint called up his 3rd Battalion to envelop the enemy positions. Lieutenant-Colonel Stumpf's battalion faced similar difficulties as it tried to reach Le Ferrange, coming under heavy fire from the opposite side of the Divette valley. As the two battalions struggled to advance, occasionally firing on each other, Company K lost its way in the maze of hedgerows. The attack was a shambles and once patrols located the missing company, sheltering along the railway line under heavy crossfire, Colonel Flint ordered his battalions to regroup. A second advance was more successful but when 39th Regiment finally contacted 4th Cavalry, Colonel Flint was ordered to break off contact and to regroup behind the centre of the division:

'Regiment alerted to move, all plans for the morning changed, advised units are in action and can not be readily be alerted.'

The manoeuvre was eventually completed under cover of darkness. As 21 June drew to a close, 39th Regiment was ready to support the attack on Bois du Mont du Roc.

Despite the setback, Colonel Flint's experiences helped to determine General Collins future plan of attack. Troops advancing along the Divette stream could be subjected to crossfire from both sides of the valley and now that contact had been established between 9th and 79th Division, VII Corps would concentrate on clearing the high ground. It meant that 9th Division would have all three of its regiments available for the assault on Cherbourg.

While the rest of 9th Division manoeuvred into position, 47th Regiment probed *Kampfgruppen* Keil's positions on the east bank of the Néretz stream searching for targets for their artillery and the Air Force. German artillery and 88mm guns fired indiscriminately on 47th Regiment's patrols and although tanks and infantry were seen moving into Baudienville, Colonel Smythe's men kept their distance; Divisional headquarters was anxious not to become drawn into a battle too early.

The plan to survey the enemy lines began to pay off during the evening as patrols returned with fragments of information. Some had found documents and General Eddy's intelligence officers were able to study maps detailing the enemy strongpoints protecting Flottemanville-Hague. Engineers had also discovered that some minefields were fakes and careful probing established that the warning signs indicated what lay ahead;

Minesweeping was a slow and dangerous task.
NARA-111-SC-331135

black and white signs marked a dummy minefield while yellow and white signs meant danger. Several patrols had taken prisoners and a few had interesting stories to tell. Men from the 310th Marine Boat Fleet had been formed into Marine *Flugabwehr* Companies and sent to the front after their vessels had been scuttled. Anti-aircraft guns taken from the ships had also been pressed into action as ground support weapons.

47th Regiment managed to gather a wealth of information on the German positions but some prisoners were eager to point out that their comrades were preparing to fight. One reported a build up of troops on the high ground around Flottemanville-Hague, the Regiment's objective for 22 June. He had counted twenty tanks, and although there were only a few Panzer IVs, it was a worrying development. He had also seen no fewer than sixteen flak and four anti-tank guns dug in around the village.

Members of the French underground worked alongside Colonel Smythe's men, questioning the local population about enemy positions and strengths. General Eddy was impressed by the assistance given and to recognise their efforts the divisional staff organised US Army uniforms for their new Allies. Divisional headquarters also reported that the underground members possessed intimate knowledge of the German fortifications and 'could be a great help in planning the attack.' Many locals were anxious to help their liberators and some resorted to sabotage:

> 'Tank Destroyer officer met civilians digging up cable alongside road, probably Cherbourg – St Lo communications. Also reported two German observers dressed as civilians, carrying packs on bicycles.'

The cable was thought to be General von Schlieben's telephone link to Seventh Army Headquarters, a vital link in the German communications.

79th Division

79th Division also spent the day probing the German lines, sending out patrols to locate *Kampfgruppen* Koehn's strongpoints. The instructions given to Lieutenant Monk, an officer with 313th Regiment's 1st Battalion, were repeated all along the division's front:

> 'Two radio towers are dominant guide features on the terrain. It is reported that there are two gun emplacements near those

Lieutenant Monk's patrol was ambushed as it reconnoitred a German communications centre. NARA-111-SC-200572

towers. The mission of your patrol is to find out whether there are Germans in the area around the radio towers and to get the information back. Use the stream as your guide. Stress concealment and watch out for German positions. If there are Germans there, find out how many there are there. You are to get information back, but fight if you have to.'

Patrolling the narrow lanes and fields was nerve-wracking work and although the Germans usually relied on artillery and small arms fire to deter the American patrols, the GIs occasionally encountered their opposite number. Fire fights amongst the lanes and hedgerows were brief and bloody as each patrol endeavoured to overwhelm their enemy. After locating two camouflaged artillery pieces, Lieutenant Monk's patrol was on its way back to safety when it stumbled on a German patrol:

'Upon return trip, patrol was ambushed by a counter patrol of at least five men, four of whom were behind a hedgerow and

the other to the right flank of the patrol. Enemy patrol cornered and four killed by M-1 fire. Lieutenant Monk wounded by grenades thrown and one man of patrol possibly killed, two others injured. Lieutenant Monk arrived back in an unconscious state. Lieutenant Monk reported position of guns.'

By nightfall General Wyche was under no illusions. Patrols were reporting pillboxes, gun positions, machine gun nests and wire entanglements all along the front, 2nd Battalion alone faced sixteen pillboxes. Information gleaned from the local population completed the picture; 79th Division faced one of the strongest sections of the Cherbourg fortifications.

4th Division

While the rest of VII Corps had come up against the Cherbourg Landfront, 4th Division had not found the main line of resistance covering the area southeast of the city. General Barton was anxious to locate the German fortifications so he would be ready to assault the fortified area alongside the rest of the Corps.

8th Regiment attacked first, aiming to clear *Kampfgruppen* Koehn's outposts in Bois de Roudou. Heavy resistance was expected in the heart of the woods where reconnaissance planes had reported a large construction site:

'... a large unfinished German installation, apparently a Buzz-Bomb site. There were a large number of concrete dugouts

The Cotentin Peninsula was an ideal base for Hitler's V1 Rocket campaign against the south coast of England.

An aerial view of the huge installation. NARA-111-SC-190780-S

north west of the crossroads while all the surrounding houses were strongly defended. A number of 88's were in position near the crossroads.'

1st and 3rd Battalions cleared scattered outposts on the outskirts of the wood but as they moved closer to the construction site, 88mm and 20mm AA guns brought the advance to a standstill. Dense undergrowth prevented Colonel Van Fleet using his armour and the divisional artillery failed to silence the gun positions. Eventually, 3rd Battalion tried to outflank the position and had advanced 800 metres before it was spotted. German infantry quickly pinned Lieutenant-Colonel Strickland's men down bringing the attempt to clear the wood to an end.

While the rest of he Regiment battled their way through Bois du Rondou, 2nd Battalion attacked Crossroads 148, to the northeast. To begin with Lieutenant-Colonel MacNeely's advance showed some promise as Company E advanced through a gap in enemy lines while the Germans sheltered from the mortar and artillery bombardment. Company G ran into a nest of concrete bunkers and before long heavy fire from three sides had pinned it down, splitting 2nd Battalion's attack in two. After calling for armoured support MacNeely brought forward the battalion's anti-tank guns and machine guns to give covering fire while Company F prepared to break the deadlock using unusual tactics:

'Marched on La Bourdonnerie; had a severe fight. Here MacNeely used attack formation of tank platoon in line, an infantry platoon immediately behind each tank (Co HQ behind the fifth tank). The whole line charged, tanks firing guns and machine-guns, infantry spraying with all their machine-guns. It was the goddamnest looking formation; I held my breath when I saw Company F line up behind those tanks but it was successful.'

As the tanks rumbled forward with Company F tucked in behind, the Germans fled. A high explosive shell damaged one tank, ripping off a track, but the rest escorted MacNeely's men safely as far as Company E. Unfortunately, Colonel MacNeely knew nothing of the hold up in Bois du Rondou and his success

8th Regiment found heavily guarded V1 installations in Bois du Rondou

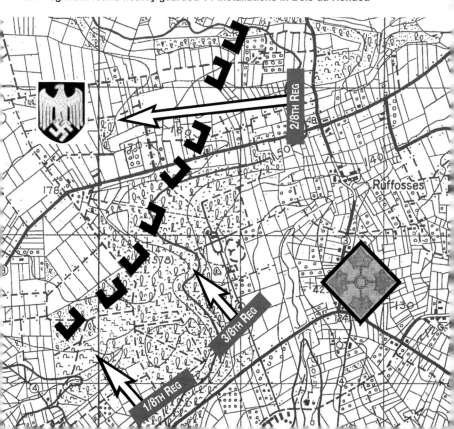

left his battalion isolated from the rest of the Regiment. Rather than withdraw and risk heavy casualties, 2nd Battalion dug in for the night, expecting the Germans holding Crossroads 148 to withdraw. They were mistaken. German troops closed in on MacNeely's perimeter during the night, making it impossible for supply trucks to get through. 2nd Battalion was cut off.

12th Infantry Regiment had moved into the centre of 4th Division's line during the night. At first light, 2nd Battalion moved forward towards Bois du Coudray, a thick belt of woods over a mile long and half a mile wide. After wading across the stream skirting the edge of the wood, the GIs plunged into the thick undergrowth finding only a handful of snipers. Moving cautiously forward, it soon became clear that the snipers had been acting as lookouts for the main German position. As 2nd Battalion reached the northern edge of the wood, the GIs found a second stream, the Saire, blocked their way and heavy fire greeted the leading company as it emerged from the trees. *Kampfgruppen* Rohrbach had made use of a natural gap in the woods, positioning bunkers on the far bank overlooking the marshy ground either side of the stream. Tanks could not cross the stream and the only bridge in the area had already been destroyed. As Colonel Luckett learned of the natural barrier, artillery and mortars began to zero in on 2nd Battalion, proving that the Germans were determined to hold the stream. With daylight fading, all Luckett could do was order the rest of his Regiment into the woods, ready to begin the search for a crossing further downstream at first light.

With two of his Regiments bogged down in front of the German outpost line, General Barton was hoping that Lieutenant-Colonel Hervey A Tribolet might be able to break the deadlock. The plan for 22nd Regiment was an ambitious one, based on the hope that *Kampfgruppen* Rohrbach had withdrawn from the area north of Le Thiel. Barton wanted his men to drive north at speed, skirting the belt of fortifications east of Cherbourg, and cut the road connecting Cherbourg and St Pierre Église. The move would isolate any Germans gathering in the northeast tip of the Cotentin peninsula and in particular around Maupertus Airfield, a suspected strongpoint.

In the late afternoon 1st and 3rd Battalions moved out from Le Theil and as the infantry pushed north their artillery shelled likely targets on the road ahead. To begin with it looked as

An anti-tank platoon heads north through a ruined village. NARA-111-SC-190401

though the Germans had withdrawn but as the head of the column reached Pinabel, artillery stationed around Maupertus airfield opened fire. Colonel Tribolet had expected to dig in for the night at Pinabel but Hill 158, the highest point on the road between Cherbourg and St Pierre Église, overlooked the hamlet. As 22nd Regiment moved nearer anti-aircraft guns opened fire but rather than withdrawing to a safer distance, Tribolet requested permission to push on in the hope of taking Hill 158. General Collins approved the suggestion and as the light faded 22nd Regiment advanced.

Elements of 729th Infantry Regiment unable to reach Cherbourg had headed towards Maupertus airfield with the intention of making a last stand and many of the soldiers were hardened fanatics intent on fighting to the end. Their positions around the landing strip were backed up by an impressive array of artillery and AA guns and they prevented Tribolet's 1st Battalion from reaching the airfield. However, 3rd Battalion infiltrated the outposts covering Hill 158 under cover of darkness and by midnight the rest of the Regiment had reached the summit. General Barton and General Collins were delighted to hear that 22nd Regiment had taken the hilltop position:

'It was a strongly fortified position containing a radio tower

63

Cherbourg

St Pierre Eglise

Maupe Airfi

22ND REGIMENT

Hill 158

22nd Regiment's daring dash to Hill 158 cut Maupertus airfield off from the rest of *Festung* Cherbourg. The Regiment formed a circular perimeter.

and was the centre of communication for the fortified area to the west and northwest. The Corps Commander attached great importance to the position and gave special congratulations to the division on accomplishment of this mission.'

The advance left 22nd Regiment with an extended supply line and throughout the night it became apparent that German troops were intent on attacking anything moving along the road to Le Thiel. 2nd Battalion spent the night trying to secure the road but as soon as the American patrols passed by, the Germans would reappear:

'Germans in considerable force, but apparently unorganised, infiltrated across their rear continually during the next four days and nights. Communication during this period was uncertain. Sometimes a single man would succeed in moving between the forward and rear elements without difficulty, at other times a considerable party would be stopped completely.'

Tanks loaded with supplies managed to escort 3rd Battalion's convoy as far as Hill 158 but 1st Battalion's supply trucks had to turn back; it was a problem that would persist for several days.

CHAPTER SIX

22 June – The first assault

On the morning of 19 June the capture of Cherbourg had taken on a greater urgency as the weather across the English Channel took a turn for the worse. Strong winds combined with high tides began to whip up heavy seas, pounding the Normandy coast with huge waves. By noon it had become too dangerous to unload supplies and equipment directly onto the beaches and personnel had to be evacuated from the outer breakwater of the temporary harbour on Omaha Beach. By nightfall the wind speed had increased to 30 knots, driving smaller craft into rocks and onto the beaches; ninety would eventually be left stranded on the shoreline. The following day the floating breakwater broke its moorings, and as the troops watched helplessly from the shore the huge bombardons were sent crashing into the harbour piers before they finally beached on the shore.

While waves continued to batter the Normandy coastline, VII

An aerial view of Fort du Roule, note the gun embrasures on the cliff face.
NARA-111-SC-191502

Corps' headquarters had begun to plan the final assault on Cherbourg. As the infantry reports on the enemy fortifications protecting Cherbourg continued to flood in, General Collins was preparing a coordinated air and ground assault for the afternoon of 22 June. Although the availability and timing of the air strikes depended very much on the weather, planning still went ahead. In the meantime, General Collins explored the possibility of negotiating surrender terms and teams armed with loudspeakers broadcast messages in German, French, Polish and Russian throughout the night.

VII Corps plan envisaged all three divisions breaking through the outer perimeter of fortifications before closing in on the port. 9th Division's main thrust would be made on its right flank, taking Octeville village and the heights overlooking the port from the southwest. Meanwhile, Collins wanted 79th Division to push north astride the Cherbourg highway, heading for Fort du Roule, a Napoleonic fort situated on a narrow cliff to the south of the city. On the right flank 4th Division was to drive northeast to seize the high ground overlooking Tourlaville before heading for the coast. On 21 June, General Collins issued his verbal orders to all three divisional commanders, stressing the need for urgency:

'This attack on Cherbourg is the major effort of the American Army and is especially vital now that unloading across the beaches has been interfered with by weather. All Division Commanders surely appreciate the importance of this attack.'

As the three General's went away to plan their attacks, the storm continued to batter Omaha beach and that night rough seas swept away the port's pier heads and buckled the bridging connecting the piers to the shore. Attempts to bring ammunition ashore continued but so far only a few small coasters beached at low tide could be unloaded. First Army needed Cherbourg to ensure success in Normandy but the conditions on the beaches was reaching crisis point. As VII Corps prepared to launch its attack, General Bradley announced that ammunition stocks were far below the recommended level; General Collins' would have to reduce his artillery expenditure by one third.

On the morning of 22 June, the winds began to abate, but supplies would not be able to be landed until the following morning. Following reports that the storm had only registered Force 6 and more bad weather could follow, Admiral Hall, the naval commander in charge of the Omaha beachhead, decided that rebuilding the ravaged artificial port was impractical. Materials designated to repair the artificial harbour would be redirected to Arromanches in the British sector, a reinforced outer breakwater would be built at Omaha to protect craft from heavy seas.

On the morning of 22 June the weather appeared favourable for air support and at 09:00 Major-General Elwood R Quesada of the IX Tactical Air Command was able to confirm that over 1,000 planes were available. As the ultimatum to the commander of the German forces had expired, General Collins informed his three divisional generals that the aerial bombardment would start at 12:40; 9th and 79th Divisions would advance at 14:00, while 4th Division would follow thirty minutes later. Although the final planning had been carried out at General Collins headquarters in Normandy, many of the aircraft were still operating from across the Channel leaving little time to fly the plans over to England and distribute them to the squadron leaders. Many last minute changes never reached the pilots and although VII Corps intended to pull back over half a mile from the German positions, the GIs would soon find out what it was like to be under attack from the air.

The Air Attack

Throughout the morning all three divisions moved their men and vehicles back to their assembly areas and as zero hour approached white phosphorous shells were fired to mark the bombing line. As four squadrons of Typhoons and six squadrons of Mustangs flew over, the infantry lit yellow flares to indicate their positions while vehicles displayed yellow panels. Despite the precautions some pilots became

Typhoons, armed with rockets, prepare to take off to attack targets in support of the Normandy invasion.

disorientated and as the wind blew the flares across the countryside, radio reports started to flood in; the planes were attacking friendly troops. Casualties were light but the Air Force nearly scored an embarrassing 'own goal' in 9th Division's area. Several planes had failed to notice the warning signs on 60th Regiment's front and while fighters strafed the infantry, two bombs fell in 2nd Battalion's deployment area. When Major Welch visited 60th Regiment's command post seeking information on the 'friendly fire', Colonel Rohan was able to give him a first hand report. A stray fighter had strafed the regimental command post sending General Eddy and the Colonel diving for cover.

In 47th Regiment's sector, Colonel Smythe's men noticed that the smoke was beginning to drift across their lines and although urgent calls for extra flares were made, they arrived too late to divert the bombers and fighters:

> 'Positions in front of the Regiment were bombed every five minutes by dive bombers for one hour and then medium bombers hit to the rear of the objective. Several bombs fell in Battalion area causing some casualties. Planes with Allied markings bombed and strafed our elements.'

Eight 500lb bombs were dropped on 1st Battalion's positions and 2nd Battalion cursed the Air Force as the planes bombed and strafed their assembly area. A few pilots became completely disorientated and began strafing 89th Artillery Battalion, several thousand metres behind the Allied lines!

Once the fighters had completed their mission, the first of twelve groups of fighter-bombers of the Ninth Air Force, flew over the Cotentin Peninsula. For fifty-five minutes over 550 P-47's, P-38's, and P-51's bombed and strafed strongpoints all along VII Corps' front and yet again some planes mistook the American troops for enemy concentrations.

Despite the mistakes made, the fighters and bombers had caused few casualties and many GIs must have wondered how effective the attacks had been on the German strongpoints. They would not have long to wait. As the last wave of fighter-bombers disappeared into the distance, VII Corps began its assault, supported by every available artillery piece. Meanwhile, nearly 400 medium and heavy bombers began to target eleven defensive positions on the hills surrounding Cherbourg.

A 155mm Howitzer shells the German positions. NARA-111-SC-190792-S

9th Division

General Eddy wanted 60th Regiment to advance towards *Kampfgruppen* Keil's positions on the high ground northwest of Flottemanville-Hague and while 1st Battalion attacked strongpoints on the ridge overlooking Acqueville, 2nd Battalion would clear Hill 150 north of the village. Meanwhile, Colonel Rohan still had to guard his left flank from German counterattacks. Overnight reports of infantry and vehicles

The advance begins; a GI races past a signpost for Cherbourg-West.

assembling near Ste Croix-Hague had made it necessary to deploy 3rd Battalion near the coast, covering the Regiment's open flank.

Colonel Rohan had left Lieutenant-Colonel Cox in no doubt what he expected, telling him 'if you run into anything don't fail to use artillery. A lot depends on this.' 1st Battalion bypassed Acqueville and although machine guns and mortars on Hill 150 opened fire, Lieutenant-Colonel Cox ordered his men to push on, expecting 2nd Battalion to clear up the flank. Crossroads 133 lay ahead and a strongpoint covering the junction came to life as 1st Battalion drew close. Cox's men fanned out around the nest of bunkers, engaging snipers, while tank-destroyers moved forward to engage the machine gun nests and mortar pits. For over an hour the infantry worked closely with the armour, locating entrenchments for the tank crews. A report on tactics written after the battle illustrates how infantry and armour had to work together to be successful:

'The tank destroyers should remain in rear of the assault battalion areas. When a suitable target is found, the platoon leader or gun commander should go forward and reconnoitre gun positions and route thereto, before bringing the gun forward. When the target is reduced, the tank destroyer should withdraw to a position in the rear of the infantry until a new target is found. Under no circumstances should the guns advance until the infantry has proceeded and located targets. A very effective weapon when thus properly employed.'

Progress was slow and 1st Battalion finally cleared Crossroads 129 as it began to grow dark. Meanwhile, 2nd Battalion had fallen behind, leaving Hill 150 in German hands. Little had been heard from Lieutenant-Colonel Kauffman during the afternoon and when he was finally contacted, Colonel Rohan discovered that 2nd Battalion had misinterpreted his orders:

'White [2nd Battalion] *thought he wasn't to move fast, but he now is. He thinks he is in reserve. He is now supposed to move fast so get message to him as fast as possible. He is supposed to pull abreast of Red [1st Battalion].'*

With 2nd Battalion moving up its flank, 1st Battalion was able to turn its full attentions to a counterattack developing along its front. The Regiment's Canon Company did not help matters and persisting in shelling Cox's positions as his men struggled to keep the Germans at bay.

Pillboxes formed the backbone of the ring of fortifications surrounding Cherbourg. NARA-111-SC-191315

2nd Battalion ran into difficulties as it made its way across Hill 150 and attempts to outflank entrenchments covering Crossroads 129 were thwarted by a bunker on Hill 160. As darkness fell, Colonel Rohan began to realise that his left flank was at a standstill and his two battalions had still failed to make contact. Both of his battalions were requesting armoured support but the tank crews were finding it difficult to distinguish friend from foe amongst the hedgerows. One tank working with 1st Battalion became disorientated and began firing on 2nd Battalion's positions; Kauffman's curt message to the Regimental Command post sums up his frustration, 'Tell tank with Red [1st Battalion] to quit shelling my men.'

General Eddy was far from happy by 60th Regiment's progress and made his feelings known during a visit to Colonel Rohan's headquarters:

'General Eddy visited command post. Want to know what tanks are doing out of sector.. General displeased with progress. Wants to know what White [2nd Battalion] is doing. Did Nutmeg [Rohan] plan to ignore high ground? Cox hasn't made any advance... Wants to know what misunderstanding is. Is

General Eddy was aggravated by 60th Regiment's slow progress north of Acqueville.

resistance heavy? The left is in a mess but it is being cleared up...
Get up to Hill 180 tonight General says.'

60th Regiment's situation finally began to improve late in the evening. Colonel Rohan ordered 3rd Battalion forward, securing the high ground overlooking Acqueville on the left flank. Meanwhile, 2nd Battalion had finally reorganised and had begun moved towards the bunker on Hill 160, leaving one company behind with the tanks to clear Crossroads 129. Colonel Rohan was also relieved to hear that Lieutenant-Colonel Kauffmen was still advancing, albeit slowly, in spite of German attempts to infiltrate his lines. Following a frustrating day Colonel Rohan was finally able to report that his men had secured a firm footing on the high ground north and east of Acqueville.

47th Regiment's advance towards Crossroads 114 ran into difficulties almost as soon as it had begun. 2nd Battalion's mortars shelled Company F as it drew close to the crossroads, alerting a strongpoint. Machine gun fire raked the company's position and as the GIs spread out to locate the bunker, their company commander called for armoured support. Meanwhile, Company E had scored an early success, taking fifty-four prisoners of the 30th Flak Regiment in a series of entrenchments north of the crossroads. The artillerymen had been forced to abandon their guns during the retreat to Cherbourg and had been given rifles so they could fight as infantrymen.

3rd Battalion had also had a good start, advancing slowly through Baudienville. However, German troops dug in on the high ground beyond the Houelbecq stream spotted Lieutenant-Colonel Clayman's men as soon as they left the village. Tank-destroyers were unable to get close enough to target the strongpoints so as Colonel Smythe arranged for artillery support, Company L crawled forward covered by the battalion mortars. 1st Battalion reported it was 'moving nicely' to begin with but they soon they way barred by four belts of barbed wire and a minefield along the Houelbecq stream. Two strongpoints on the opposite bank opened fire at short range as the GIs tried to find away across.

As the hours passed, Colonel Smythe was becoming increasingly concerned by the lack of progress, all along the front casualties mounted as his men struggled to find a way through *Kampfgruppen* Keil's line. On 2nd Battalion's front, tank-destroyers knocked out one of the pillboxes at Crossroads

Tank destryoyers were particularly effective for dealing with strongpoints.

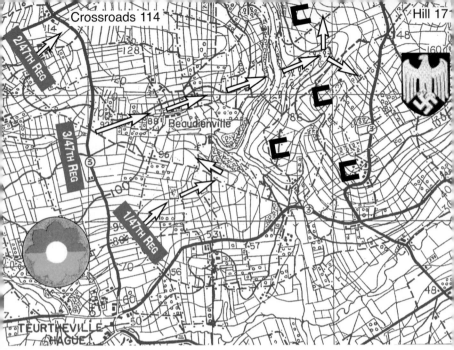

German positions east of the Houelbecq stream threatened to halt 47th Regiment's advance towards Hill 171.

114 but the remaining bunker continued to fight on. Both Companies E and F resorted to working their way around the flanks of the position, while Company G moved up from reserve. Although 2nd Battalion had started to move forward, Allied fighters strafed the Battalion as it prepared to assault Le Saussy crossroads. The attack from the air stopped the advance in its tracks.

Meanwhile, Company G had worked its way around the flank of Crossroads 114, reaching the last hedgerow behind the position before they were seen. Tank destroyers gave covering fire, targeting the pillbox's firing slits, as a platoon charged across the field and burst into the bunker finding fifty dazed soldiers inside.

Along the banks of the Houelbecq stream, Company L on 3rd Battalion's front, had started to push men onto the far bank. Attempts to cross the stream anywhere else had failed and as it began to grow dark, Colonel Smythe ordered 1st Battalion to disengage and exploit the gap. While the two battalions queued up to cross, fanning out to form a defensive perimeter on the opposite bank, Company L closed in on Strongpoint 8. As the infantry crept along the hedgerows they were relieved to see a shell hit the strongpoint's ammunition dump, rocking the bunkers with a series of explosions. The situation looked promising and although white flags started to appear, there were no other signs that the garrison intended to surrender.

As the final round of smoke shells exploded around Strongpoint 8, Company L charged up the hill, clearing the outlying entrenchments. Earlier in the day civilians had reported that the morale of the German troops was low and 'most soldiers had to be forced to fight at gunpoint' but as Company L worked its way through the strongpoint fanatics

Another German bunker silenced.
NARA-111-SC-190980

continued to fire until the last moment. Strongpoint 8 had been cleared and Lieutenant-Colonel Clayman was pleased to report that his men had found 'fifty shell shocked prisoners and the rest are deader than hell.' By midnight 47th Regiment's right flank was firmly dug in on the forward slopes of Hill 171. Ahead lay Bois du Mont du Roc and although civilians believed that *Kampfgruppen* Keil had withdrawn from the woods, Colonel Smythe was taking no chances; throughout the night 9th Division's artillery shelled likely targets on the summit of Hill 171 and in the woods beyond.

After a frustrating day General Eddy was pleased to hear that cracks were beginning to appear in the line of strongpoints covering Flottemanville-Hague and Bois du Mont du Roc. 60th Regiment had finally secured the division's left flank while 47th Regiment was firmly established on the east bank of the Houelbecq stream. There were still isolated pockets of resistance behind 9th Division's front but 39th Regiment was moving to the Baudienville area ready to round them up at first light. It meant that General Eddy could prepare for the assault on the next belt of fortifications.

79th Division

Major-General Wyche's plan for 22 June was to advance on a narrow front between the Divette and Trottebec streams with all of his three regiments. The main effort was to be made by 313th Regiment on the division's right flank astride the main highway to Cherbourg. 314th Regiment would advance onto the high ground beyond Tollevast, west of the highway while 315th Regiment contained any German forces in the Hardinvast area on the division's left flank. As the last planes flew overhead, General Wyche passed on the following words of encouragement to his subordinates, 'Gentlemen, you have the honour of striking the decisive blow for our forces. I shall see you in Cherbourg.'

Colonel Wood knew that a huge anti-tank ditch, in places four metres deep and five metres wide, straddled the Cherbourg road at les Chèvres. *Kampfgruppen* Koehn had cleared the undergrowth and trees either side of the ditch creating a killing zone for the bunkers and emplacements on the far side. 313th Regiment would have to work in close cooperation with the engineers and tanks to stand any chance of

General Eisenhower discusses the battle with General Bradley and General Wyche. NARA-111-SC-191158

A 155mm Howitzer provides close support from its camouflaged position.
NARA-111-SC-190791-S

Engineers take cover as explosives blast open the door of a bunker. Below: GIs survey the results of their work.

success and Wood's orders left no doubt in his subordinates minds what he expected, 'Don't give them a chance to recover. Don't fiddle. Shoot and use the bayonet.'

Close support from the artillery was essential and the infantry was expected to move as near as possible to the strongpoints, in some cases as little as one hundred metres, before firing double green flares to signify they were ready to attack.

Engaging the bunkers was a nerve-racking task and infantry were expected to target the pillboxes' embrasures while the engineers blew gaps in the barbed wire with pole shaped charges, known as Bangalore torpedoes. The infantry could then move up close, throwing satchel charges at the firing slits to try and concuss the men inside. Hedgerows posed a problem to the tanks and the engineers were expected to make gaps with explosives to allow them to keep up with the infantry. Each strongpoint demanded a different technique and company commanders continually faced new problems; one wrong decision and an entire platoon of men could be mown down.

On 313th Regiment's front 1st Battalion came under heavy machine gun fire as it approached les Chèvres and as three platoons of tanks moved forward, Lieutenant-Colonel Clair B Mitchell took stock of his position. Camouflaged anti-tank guns opened fire as the tanks came into view, destroying one and disabling a second and as the rest of the Shermans withdrew to a safe distance, Colonel Wood had to admit that his advance was stalled. 1st Battalion withdrew to regroup and while the artillery shelled the German positions, Wood decided to try and find a weak point in the *Kampfgruppen* Koehn's line.

3rd Battalion deployed to the west of the highway and after probing the German lines found a way across the anti-tank ditch and manoeuvred into position close to the strongpoints blocking the highway. An air strike by fighter-bombers paved the way and as 3rd Battalion closed in on the flank of the German position, Colonel Wood led 1st Battalion across the anti-tank ditch:

'The Old Man, his executive officer Lieutenant-Colonel Edwin M Van Bibber, and other key officers of the regimental staff personally led infantry assault teams across fields, fighting their way from hedgerow to hedgerow after dive-bombers had made their low level attack on the first line of German forts. The

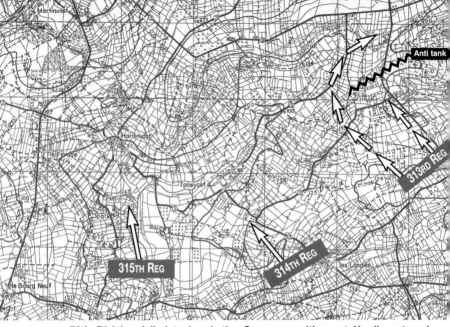

79th Division failed to break the German positions at Hardinvast and Tollevast but 313th Regiment exploited a weak point to the west of Les Chèvres.

Old Man took his men up so fast they bypassed the largest fort before its defenders knew what the score was. The assault teams closed in with bangalore torpedoes and flamethrowers, catching the Germans in the rear and cleaning them out of the fort as either corpses or prisoners in short order.'

As the two battalions cleared bunker after bunker enemy mortars fired on a position when a white flag appeared. It appeared that some fanatics would go to any lengths to hold les Chèvres. Casualties were heavy but Colonel Wood's men had broken a key position on the road to Cherbourg. As darkness fell and the last prisoners were being escorted to the rear the engineers began to bulldoze a road across the ditch.

314th Regiment had experienced its own difficulties and 1st Battalion spent the afternoon pinned down in front of Tollevast. Attempts to outflank the village failed as the GIs stumbled on hidden positions. 315th Regiment also failed to advance towards Hardinvast and as daylight faded General Wyche considered how to exploit the breakthrough at les Chèvres.

Colonel Wood was instructed to send his men deep into the German lines under cover of darkness and while 3rd Battalion advanced to the west of the Cherbourg highway, 1st Battalion crossed the road with 2nd Battalion echeloned behind its right

313th Regiment take up positions around Crossroads 177; the German signpost gives directions to Cherbourg East.

flank. Corps artillery paved the way, allowing the two leading battalions to press on as far as Crossroads 177, a commanding position far behind *Kampfgruppen* Koehn's front line. 2nd Battalion ran into difficulties in the woods northeast of les Chèvres and control disintegrated as the GIs engaged in running battles among the trees; it would be daylight before the battalion reorganised and joined the rest of the Regiment.

As 313th Regiment pushed north, General Wyche ordered Colonel Robinson to disengage and move towards les Chèvres, 315th Regiment would eventually take over responsibility for patrolling the Tollevast sector. Having battered one hole through the German lines, Wyche had no intentions of making another; 314th Regiment would follow 313th Regiment to Crossroads 177.

Following a disappointing afternoon, Major-General Wyche was able to report that over half his strength had established a sizeable foothold one mile inside the enemy positions. Tanks had been sent up to support the forward position but German patrols were still operating behind 79th Division's lines making it too dangerous to send soft vehicles forward. So far Oberst Koehn was unaware that the crossroads had been taken; 23 June

81

was going to be interesting day for all concerned on the road to Cherbourg.

4th Division

Throughout the night German troops had been infiltrating 8th Regiment's lines. As zero hour approached, neither the artillery nor the tanks Colonel van Fleet expected were ready, leaving the infantry to advance alone. 1st Battalion moved off an hour late and immediately ran into stiff opposition. Repeated counterattacks threatened to overrun Company A and B and Lieutenant-Colonel Simmons eventually called for assistance from the regimental artillery, ordering it to shell his own positions. The barrage broke the German onslaught and as they withdrew, 1st Battalion occupied its objective taking one hundred prisoners. The GIs could not fail to notice the mixture of uniforms amongst their captives. Tank crews, anti-aircraft and searchlight troops, military police and naval personnel were all mingled in with the infantry from 709th Infantry Division; it was a sure sign that General von Schlieben was using every available man to defend Cherbourg.

3rd Battalion also advanced without their tanks or artillery, moving quickly past a V1 rocket installation. There was little sign of the enemy and Lieutenant-Colonel Strickland began to wonder if his men had found a weak point in *Kampfgruppen* Koehn's line. It was merely the lull before the storm. As Company L ran from one hedgerow to the next, flak guns and machine guns opened fire from hidden positions:

'The Germans had cut lanes of fire with notches in the hedgerows cleared of trees and bushes. These lanes were concealed so they were not obvious from the front. The enemy held their fire until the attacking troops were a perfect target, then opened fire and inflicted heavy casualties.'

With Company L pinned down and unable to disengage, Strickland ordered Company I to work its way through a copse to outflank of the strongpoint. The Germans were waiting for them:

'The Germans placed a heavy artillery barrage on the wood and the tree bursts produced a terrific effect, heavy shells bursting in the trees about ten feet form the ground. Company I lost 54 men in this barrage.'

For several hours Strickland's men fought for their lives as they

82

tried to escape the German guns and regroup. When Company C, 70th Tank Battalion, many hours later than expected, the sound of the Sherman tanks crawling along the lanes broke the Germans' will to fight. As they withdrew, Strickland's men occupied the entrenchments and counted their losses. Another German position had fallen, but at a terrible cost. 3rd Battalion had suffered thirty-one killed and ninety-two wounded; eleven of them were officers.

2nd Battalion had spent the night dug in north of Bois du Rondou, cut off from the rest of the Regiment. Lieutenant-Colonel MacNeely had expected the German troops holding Crossroads 148 to his rear to withdraw under cover of darkness, but instead they went on the offensive during the early hours of the morning. Yet again, German troops displayed their infiltration skills, harassing Lieutenant-Colonel MacNeely's men and they eventually stole five machine guns from the battalion command post. The menace around Crossroads 148, had to be dealt with before 2nd Battalion could advance and at first light Captain Kulp's company (numbering only ninety strong), was ordered to return to Crossroads 148 to deal with the enemy position:

An aerial view of Crossroads 148, the woods to the north were a hive of construction activity.

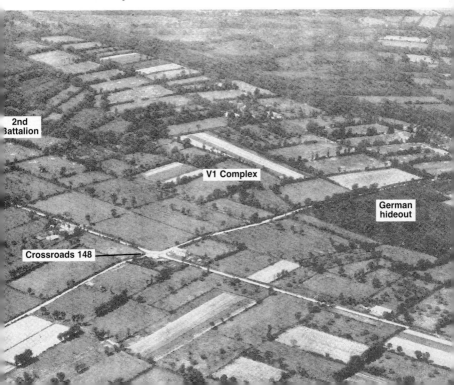

'I receive the order at 06:45; it was not until four hours later that I attacked. I didn't know what they had back there but I knew it was strong. I wanted to keep them from knowing that if I could.'

Kulp and Lieutenant Dooley watched as dozens of Germans emerged from fortified houses clustered around the crossroads and disappeared into a small wood to avoid detection. Rather than stage an assault, Kulp ordered his company to encircle the hiding place; he had decided to show the Germans that his own men were also capable of infiltration:

'Leaving the 2nd Platoon in its frontal position, he moved his first platoon behind the hedgerows into a concealed position where they could look down into the woods from the northeast. With the 1st Platoon were two .50 calibre machine guns and three .03 calibre machine guns. The 81mm mortars were in position and trained on the woods; fire support from the cannon company was arranged for the same woods. Meanwhile, the 3rd Platoon was making a wide flanking move, going south through the large woods and up the draw.'

American artillery in action, the message on the shell reads 'Fireworks for Hitler'. NARA-111-SC-191155

Mortars helped to shatter the German position at Crossroads 148.

As soon as Captain Kulp saw Lieutenant Williams and 3rd Platoon approaching the crossroads from the south, he gave the order to fire. A cease-fire was called eight minutes later. Eighty 105mm shells and over 1,000 mortar rounds had raked the wood from end to end while thousands of machine gun bullets had caused consternation among the trees:

> *'You know how bullets sound in woods; it sounds like they are coming from everywhere. The moment the firing ceased, white flags appeared everywhere and yells of "Kamerad" came*

Machine guns completed the devastation.

from all sides. Out of the woods came seventy-four Germans and surrendered. When the flow of prisoners seemed to have stopped, Kulp opened fire on the woods again. After the second operation, more Heinies [American slang based on Heineken, the German beer] *came out of the dugouts and fortified houses and out of the woods. When we thought they had all come, by God if 100 didn't come from down the road from the fortification.'*

Captain Kulp's men eventually rounded up 244 prisoners and found another fifty dead; Company F had no casualties.

Having secured his rear, Lieutenant-Colonel MacNeely turned his attention to the fortifications on the northern edge of Bois du Rondou. 2nd Battalion engaged a number of large bunkers with flamethrowers, Bangalore torpedoes and the 105mm howitzers of the Cannon Company, securing the Regiment's right flank by nightfall. 8th Regiment had taken a large number of prisoners during the advance but Colonel van Fleet's men had paid the price; 249 had been killed or wounded in the hedgerows north of Bois du Rondou.

12th Regiment's advance had been brought to a sudden halt

12th Regiment's attempt to break free from Bois du Coudray ended in failure.

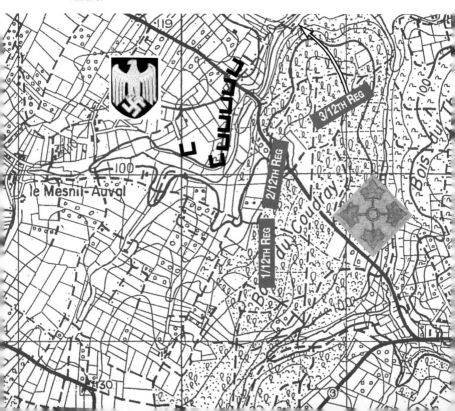

The moment of surrender captured by the cameraman.

on 21 June by a series of strongpoints covering the Saire stream on the western edge of Bois du Coudray. At first light Colonel Luckett ordered his 3rd Battalion to find a crossing suitable for tanks so that they could outflank the German position. Heading north, Lieutenant-Colonel Dulin's first attempt to cross the stream failed in the face of heavy machine gun fire. At a second crossing two companies waded through the stream and charged up the far bank to find twenty German soldiers, many of them Labour Corps personnel, with their hands up. Although 3rd Battalion had established a footing on the far side of the stream, the Shermans were unable to cross; Dulin's men would have to go on alone. They had only advanced a short distance when a hidden strongpoint opened fire, splitting the battalion in half. Two companies were pinned down close to the German position and unable to manoeuvre around its flanks, while the rest of the battalion was lost in the hedgerows. By the time 3rd Battalion had grouped, it was growing dark leaving Dulin no option but to withdraw to safe distance and regroup. The GIs received a shock when they discovered that German troops had already occupied a hill to their rear, cutting the battalion off from the rest of the Regiment. Lieutenant-Colonel Dulin gathered his men

German troops infiltrated VII Corps supply lines many times. Here, jeeps make their way to the front through a ruined village. NARA-111-SC-190821

together to drive the enemy back, advancing up the slope in the darkness; Dulin was killed leading the final bayonet charge. Captain Linder rallied the battalion, driving the Germans from the hill. Tired, hungry and surrounded, 3rd Battalion's survivors dug in and waited for daylight; for a second time 12th Regiment had failed to shake itself free from Bois du Coudray.

Later that evening Colonel Luckett sent tanks forward with his supply trucks, taking machine gun and mortar ammunition to 2nd Battalion. 3rd Battalion would have to wait for their supplies; Captain Linder was able to report that his men could hold their positions until the following day in spite of heavy casualties. 12th Regiment needed to push tanks across the Saire stream as soon as possible to stand a chance of advancing beyond Bois du Coudray. Throughout the night patrols searched for a way through the maze of hedgerows, only to return with bad news; many of the lanes had been heavily mined while others were too narrow for tanks. The search went on – a way across had to be found.

CHAPTER SEVEN

23 June – Making inroads into the perimeter

9th Division

As General Eddy prepared for the assault on the main German line covering Flottemanville-Hague and Bois du Mont du Roc, his men tried to sleep in their shallow foxholes. Rain added to their misery, and to many it seemed that the battle for the hedgerows and hills in front of Cherbourg would never end:

> 'The troops were on the verge of physical exhaustion after many days of bitter exertion. Nerves were jumpy, tempers raw. The Germans were still firing every gun and field piece on the peninsula directly at him, it seemed to the average foot slogger, when he peered out of his foxhole or through a hedgerow. His disgust was profound. His body revolted at the thought of the increasing pace of the campaign and the tenacity of the enemy.

'Star and Stripes' boosted the troops morale with up to date news.
NARA-111-SC-190598

*His mind was sick from the sight and smell of blood and death
mingled in with the damp earth about him. Yet his fighting spirit
and sense of duty drove him on when and where further
advances seemed impossible.'*

Meanwhile, patrols on 47th Regiment's front had captured
German documents listing *Kampfgruppen* Keil's Order of Battle.
It gave a revealing insight into the state of the German troops
protecting Cherbourg. Alongside the expected Army formations
were details of miscellaneous units, composing of Naval
personnel, artillerymen and anti-aircraft crews converted into
infantry to bolster their numbers. Garrison troops and service
personnel, many of them foreign soldiers of dubious fighting
quality, had also been pressed into service and the report urged
officers to use German nationals on essential duties, in
particular night patrolling. The report's conclusions showed
that there was still a shortage of men and ammunition:

*'Short on ammunition – ordered to fire only on specific
targets. Also short of men – attempt deception by dispersing
only a few men in each bunker and spreading out thinly.'*

Throughout the night supply lorries and rear echelon units had
come under attack from isolated groups of Germans still
operating behind 9th Division's lines. At first light patrols of the
39th Regiment assisted by members of the French underground
worked alongside the American troops as they searched the
lanes and fields for their enemy. Colonel Flint's 1st Battalion
moved onto Hill 128 to clear a strongpoint behind 60th
Regiment. Company A crawled up to the hedgerow in front of
the bunkers and while it drew the Germans' fire, Company C
worked its way around the flank. The operation took most of
the day but by nightfall the battalion had cleared Hill 128 and
taken seventy-five prisoners.

German artillery observers spotted 2nd Battalion as it headed
towards the entrenchments on Hill 138 and Hill 150 but despite
the shelling the two strongpoints remained silent. A French
guide directed Company E and their supporting armour along
the narrow lanes bringing them close to the entrenchments on
Hill 138 and as soon as Lieutenant-Colonel Tucker's men were
in place, the tank-destroyers opened fire, giving the signal for
the attack. Tucker's men charged across the fields to reach the
bunkers, weaving their way through a minefield:

'Lieutenant Denny led attack through barbed wire and hit by

machine-gun pistol in shoulder and hand. Veritable arsenal just lack of men to man them.'

Company G used similar tactics to silence the enemy positions on Hill 150 and by the time it was dark 60th Regiment's rear was secure.

While 39th Regiment cleared the isolated strongpoints to its rear, 60th Regiment continued to advance towards Flottemanville-Hague. 1st Battalion's initial attack on Hill 180 was met with small arms fire and the two leading companies fell back in confusion. After regrouping a second attempt secured the summit, clearing a number of machine guns pits and a bunker housing a 50mm anti-tank gun. Artillery and mortars began to target the battalion as it advanced towards Strongpoint 13 and casualties mounted:

'... receiving heavy direct fire from high ground. Being hit from all sides. Need litter bearers.'

As Colonel Rohan's men drew closer they could see six light tanks moving into position around the strongpoint. It looked as if *Oberstleutenant* Keil was preparing to make a stand.

2nd Battalion had also been working its way steadily towards the summit of the ridge, but a counterattack had left Lieutenant-Colonel Kauffmen's men low on ammunition. With one

An ambulance transports wounded through a ruined village.
NARA-111-SC-255627

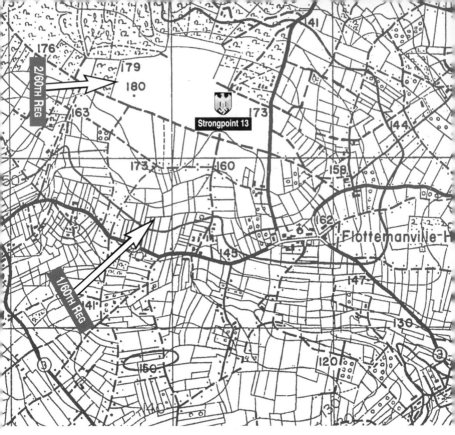

60th Regiment's advance towards Hill 180 and Strongpoint 13.

battalion pinned down and a second in danger of being cut off, 60th Regiment's attack was faltering but as Colonel Rohan prepared to commit his 3rd Battalion, Lieutenant-Colonel Kauffman reported that *Kampfgruppen* Keil had started to evacuate Hill 180. The withdrawal gave 60th Regiment the chance to reorganise and while the divisional artillery targeted suspected enemy positions, 2nd Battalion was able to occupy Hill 180.

One objective had been taken, but a rearguard had remained behind in Strongpoint 13 to delay 1st Battalion's advance. One artillery fire mission had already been cancelled following reports that patrols had entered the strongpoint. The information was incorrect and as General Eddy made arrangements with the Air Force, he left Colonel Rohan in no doubt what he expected:

'General Eddy is concerned that 1st Battalion is taking

*vicious artillery concentration from 13, see it is overrun
otherwise mortars will continue. I personally want to see the
bombing mission is followed up.'*

The dive-bombers eventually flew over as it began to grow dark
and 60th Regiment advanced as the artillery bombarded
Strongpoint 13. German rearguards fired on Colonel Rohan's
men as they advanced along the ridge but 1st Battalion was
finally able to reach strongpoint under cover of darkness. Tank-
destroyers followed and engaged bunkers and emplacements
while the infantry cleared out the maze of trenches, taking
thirty-seven dazed prisoners. General Eddy was elated to hear
that the position had fallen. It meant that 9th Division's flank
was finally secure; his men could concentrate on closing in on
the final ring of forts protecting Cherbourg and, and in his
words, 'shoot the works'.

47th Regiment began its attack on Bois du Mont du Roc at
dawn, but as 3rd Battalion moved forward the mortar platoon
came under fire from a strongpoint behind its lines. The position
had been overlooked the previous evening and while Company
B pushed on, the rest of the battalion headed back to deal with
the emplacement. Despite the interruption, Colonel Clayman
was pleased to hear that his men had cleared a number of
bunkers with the help of tank-destroyers, taking the summit of
Hill 171.

2nd Battalion also found German troops operating to their
rear. A company of infantry revealed themselves at first light
and they had destroyed a number of supply trucks on the

Artillery had difficulty finding suitable firing positions in the 'bocage'.
NARA-111-SC-190385-S

Octeville road before they were taken prisoner. The Battalion command post also came under fire when a hidden anti-tank gun made its presence felt. The attacks delayed 2nd Battalion's advance and it was late afternoon before Colonel Smythe was confident that Hill 171 was secure.

Although progress had been slow, General Eddy was able to report that his men had secured the two highest points in the area, Hill 180 and Hill 171. 39th Regiment had finished clearing the division's rear area and once Colonel Flint had assembled his men on the Division's right flank, all three Regiment's were ready to join the final drive on Cherbourg.

79th Division

Four battalions had penetrated deep into *Kampfgruppen* Koehn's lines during the night, establishing a sizeable foothold on the high ground around Crossroads 177. There was a great deal of confusion behind 79th Division's lines as the Germans realised what had happened and their patrols spent the night attacking vehicles as they moved north along the Cherbourg highway. During the early hours Colonel Wood heard reports that the enemy had reoccupied a number of bunkers at les Chèvres, cutting off the Division's supply line. It was a serious oversight.

As it grew, light Colonel Wood was perturbed to hear that 2nd Battalion had become separated from the rest of 313th Regiment. Lieutenant-Colonel Bode could only account for seventy of his men, the rest were engaged in a futile battle along the banks of the Trottebec stream. As Bode searched the woods, trying to rally his men, a German sniper found his mark, killing the officer.

Colonel Wood was at the front line preparing for the attack on la Mare à Canards, meanwhile, back at the Regimental Command Post Major McConnell was struggling to make sense of the confusing radio reports:

'The command post consisted of a captured German Ford delivery truck and thirty foxholes, in a wet gully strewn with hay off a country lane below Hau de Haut. Neither the Old Man – the Colonel – or his staff were around.'

McConnell was sat on his folding chair in the middle of the command post, charting unit movements on a huge map board. Before long, communications were cut and Colonel Wood set off back, accompanied by two staff officers and a platoon of men, to assess the situation. As they travelled south, it was obvious that enemy patrols were still operating along the road. Major Arnaud later described the journey back through the German positions:

> 'I am telling you we came through there going like hell when we discovered the Germans had come back, unknown to us and threatened to cut us off... As we were passing a fort a German officer jumped out and yelled "surrender." I swung old Betsy [his Tommy gun] around and pulled the

Keeping a lookout for snipers in on the road to Cherbourg. NARA-111-SC-190827

trigger. When we finally got through we had killed four Jerries and taken one officer and nine enlisted men prisoners.'

The group failed to locate McConnell and his makeshift headquarters and Wood finally contacted divisional headquarters via an artillery telephone. 313th Regiment was supposed to have attacked the la Mare à Canards position at 09:30 but with no means of contacting the front line, General Wyche had concede that it would be was impossible unless Colonel Wood could recapture the reoccupied bunkers.

Stragglers formed the backbone of Wood's force and, with a platoon of tanks and a section of anti-tank guns to give supporting fire, the assault on the Chèvres position began under the watchful eye of General Wyche. It was a repeat of the previous day; only this time the tanks could cross the anti-tank ditch. As the Shermans negotiated the narrow breach, a German anti-tank gun opened fire:

> 'One tank was hit by the Germans and set afire. Its crew got out safely. Another German shell knocked the track off a second

tank, immobilising it, but the other two kept going. McCabe's
Anti-tank Company manhandled two 57s up a narrow lane into
position behind shell-scarred stumps and blasted brush, from
where they could fire on the captured fort. The Old Man was
with them, pointing out the target and directing the fire.
Gunners laid it two by two – two rounds of high explosive, then
two rounds of armour piercing shells.'

Sergeant Charles Jones drove his tank to the rear of the bunkers,
blasting the steel doors open with a dozen rounds of 75mm
armour piercing shell. One man was cut down as he tried to
make his escape, three others emerged with their hands up.
Captain John McCabe, the anti-tank section commander, later
reported what the GIs discovered inside:

'... we discovered they had a lower level of sub-basement we
didn't know about. Two groggy Germans crawled out of a hole
under one of the smaller pillboxes after we had blown its top.
There were two other dead Germans in the hole. They must have
been down there while we were in the fort. We don't know how
many may have been down there under the main fort. We
couldn't go down into its subterranean tunnels last night
because fumes from the demolition charges are poisonous. But
we think we understand now why the fort was re-manned so
quickly after we had taken it for the first time last night. After
we had passed the fort they simply came up the stairs, closed
those armour-plated doors and started to fight again. Can you
beat it?'

Lieutenant Robert C Johnson spiked the remaining 88mm gun
before blowing the bunkers to pieces with TNT charges.

314th Regiment experienced similar difficulties maintaining

Anti-tank guns engage a German strongpoint. NARA-111-SC-190399

a safe route to the rear. German troops roamed freely behind the lines, targeting supply trucks with 88mm and machine gun fire. The attacks increased as it began to grow light forcing Colonel Robinson to recall his soft vehicles until 2nd Battalion had secured the Regiment's rear. 3rd Battalion's staff were confined to their foxholes when a hidden 88mm targeted the command post; it took Major Koch and Captain West the entire morning to locate and then silence the gun position.

Despite the amount of enemy activity behind 79th Division's lines, General Wyche persevered with his plans and at 09:30 dive-bombers flew low over la Mare à Canards, targeting Strongpoint F. An artillery barrage followed, but 313th Regiment quickly found that the bombardment had failed to have the desired effect. 88s, mortars and machine guns brought Colonel Wood's advance to an abrupt halt. On 314th Regiment's front, observers could see that the fighter-bombers had missed their targets and Colonel Robinson requested a second air strike, to give his men a chance. Unfortunately, 3rd Battalion did not receive the order to wait and advanced as planned, occupying part of the objective.

In the confusion that followed, General Wyche arranged a second attack by the Air Force while company commanders tried to recall their men out of the bombing zone. In some cases the message was never received and while the artillery fired smoke 1,000 metres north of the target in the hope of diverting the planes, forty-eight P47 fighter-bombers, each carrying two 1,000lb bombs, were heading for la Mare à Canards.

Many planes heeded the smoke but a few bombed 313th Regiment's positions; putting an end to its advance. On 314th Regiment's the second air strike failed to knock out the German positions, but as 1st Battalion engaged Strongpoint F, one company penetrated a weak spot in the enemy line and pushed on alone towards La Loge, a tiny hamlet overlooking Cherbourg harbour. For the first time American troops were able to look down on their objective; finally it appeared as though the end was in sight.

4th Division

For the second night running German troops had infiltrated 8th Regiment's lines, forcing Battalion commanders to rely on their artillery to keep the enemy at bay. Poor communications and harassment of the supply lines delayed 70th Tank Battalion, leaving 1st Battalion to advance unsupported. It had only advanced a short distance when it stumbled on a strongpoint; Lieutenant-Colonel Simmons would have to wait until the Shermans arrived. 1st Battalion's progress through the maze of hedgerows was slow (it took six hours to advance 1,000 metres), and an after-action report sums up the difficulties faced by the GIs as they fought their way through the 'bocage' around Cherbourg:

'In effect, hedgerows subdivide the terrain into small rectangular compartments which favour the defence and necessitate their reduction individually by the attacker. Each compartment thus constitutes a problem in itself. On approaching such a compartment, the scouts must be particularly watchful, especially on the corners, where the enemy is frequently found commanding approaches from adjacent compartments. Fire from automatic weapons, light mortars and rifle grenades, directed at corners and along the hedgerows themselves, whether or not an enemy was known to be present therein, was found to be frequently effective.

'The entire operation resolved itself into a species of jungle or Indian fighting, in which the individual soldier or small groups of soldiers played a dominant part. Success comes to the offensive force, which employs the maximum initiative by individuals and small groups.'

While Lieutenant-Colonel Simmons' men pushed slowly west of Foret de l'Ermitage, German infantry infiltrated the battalion positions, forcing the 81mm mortar platoon to abandon their weapons. This left 1st Battalion in an exposed position close to a German strongpoint. Fearing further counterattacks, Simmons's withdrew his men to a safe distance and by nightfall his mortars were back in action.

Lieutenant-Colonel Strickland postponed his advance until 70th Tank Battalion arrived and when 3rd Battalion finally moved forward, the leading companies discovered that the Germans had been planning their own attack:

'Apparently they were in position and just about to attack when 3rd Battalion's assault hit them. As the American tanks and infantry moved through the woods and down into the draw, they found the Germans laying head to heels in the ditches and along the hedgerows. For a few minutes there was a wild melee

with shooting in all directions. Then the enemy, completely surprised and caught in the open by our tanks, were routed. The battalion drove through the fleeing Germans and killed a large number. Many of the Germans lay still in the ditches playing dead and were killed or captured by the reserve company.'

3rd Battalion took advantage of the rout and pushed north quickly but the breakthrough had not gone unnoticed. As Strickland's men advanced past a V1 installation, artillery and mortar shells began to rain down, allowing the Germans time to regroup. The advance was over and as the rest of the battalion repulsed a counterattack, one company headed back to deal with bunkers surrounding the V1 ramp. With the help of flamethrowers, Bangalore torpedoes and satchel charges Strickland's men took 228 prisoners.

In 12th Regiment's sector, Colonel Luckett finally received the piece of news that he had been waiting for. A patrol led by Sergeant Bledsoe had found an unguarded ford across the Saire stream that was suitable for tanks. At last there appeared to be a way to break the deadlock and shake free from Bois du Coudray. Bledsoe returned to the ford with seven Sherman tanks, loaded with ammunition, supplies and orders to attack, and with the help of infantry scouts they found 3rd Battalion's isolated position on the west bank of the stream.

It was too late to follow Colonel Luckett's orders as planned

An aerial view of Cherbourg harbour. Fort du Roule is on the right, perched high on a cliff top.

German infantry pause for a moment during a move to new positions.

but Captain Linder was determined to carry out the mission and turn *Kampfgruppen* Rohrbach's line. After detailing the tank scouts to look after the wounded, 3rd Battalion set out towards le Mesnil-au-Val. Hedgerows confined the Shermans to a single-track road, so Captain Linder came up with a plan to sweep the fields on the line of his advance. His men deployed either side of the road, searching for enemy positions and the whole column moved forward a field at a time. When the GIs came under fire, a tank entered the closest field to the German position and sprayed the hedges with machine gun fire, reversing back on to the road as the enemy melted away. Meanwhile, German infantry continually harried the rear of 3rd Battalion's column, forcing Linder to conduct a fighting withdrawal. Company L successfully protected the battalion's rear and when the Germans turned on the battalion aid station, medics joined the infantry to drive off the attack.

At the head of the column the Shermans scored an important success as they closed in on their objective, destroying two 88mm guns protecting a crossroads. As 3rd Battalion approached the Saire stream, the German troops opposing the rest of 12th Regiment surrendered at the sight of infantry and armour approaching from the rear and as white flags began to appear, 2nd Battalion finally waded across the steam.

Having broken the deadlock, Colonel Luckett was anxious to push towards Cherbourg before *Oberst* Rohrbach discovered the breakthrough. While 2nd Battalion cleared a number of anti-aircraft positions covering a radar installation, Luckett gave Captain Linder his new mission: he wanted him to advance towards Tourlaville. It was growing dark by the time 3rd Battalion had reorganised and using the same tactics as before, Linder's men patrolled the fields while the Shermans crawled along the road. When the light had failed, the tanks had to withdraw to rearm but Colonel Luckett urged Linder to take Hill 140, a vantage point overlooking Tourlaville.

As 3rd Battalion approached the summit of the hill, it was greeted with machine gun and mortar fire. The tanks would not be able to return until morning, so Captain Linder called on the artillery for support. The first rounds fell astride the road leading up to the German position and as Companies I and K crept as close as they dare to the line of shell bursts, Linder

GIs hunt for a sniper in the hedgerows. NARA-111-SC-191351

ordered artillery to increase their range one hundred metres at a time. Crawling forward, hugging the barrage for protection, 3rd Battalion closed in on Hill 140 until they were within striking distance. In the final charge Linder's men found many of Germans sheltering in their bunkers; another strongpoint had fallen on the road to Cherbourg.

After two days of frustration Colonel Luckett was delighted to hear that the important piece of terrain had been taken. However, *Oberst* Rohrbach was not prepared to give up the hill without a fight. Throughout the night mortars and artillery mercilessly pounded 3rd Battalion's positions, only ceasing fire to let the infantry advance. On more than one occasion Linder's men relied on their bayonets and hand grenades to drive the Germans away from their newly won position. The attacks eventually subsided in the early hours, leaving Hill 140 in the hands of 3rd Battalion.

Medics treat the wounded at a makeshift aid station. NARA-111-SC-190816

CHAPTER EIGHT

24 June – The noose tightens

On 23 June General von Schlieben had been appointed Commander in Chief of all troops in the Cherbourg area, taking over from Cherbourg's commander, *Generalmajor* Robert Sattler. Von Schlieben had requested reinforcements, but ships could not be found and Allied planes dominated the skies above Normandy; the port was cut off by land, sea and air. On the morning of 24 June, VII Corps headquarters intercepted General von Schlieben's message to Seventh Army Headquarters. It would be his last. Contact with the rest of the German forces in Normandy would be severed shortly afterwards:

'Communication with several battalions no longer available... Heavy bombers attack on Fort de Roule and flak positions... Phosphorous put eight batteries out of action. Unlikely to regroup artillery today... Tomorrow heavier attacks expected... Enemy attacks SW of Rouges Terres and Le Gilloy... Entire harbour contaminated. All informed... Completely crushed by artillery fire.'

Exhausted soldiers grab a moments rest during a lull in the fighting.
NARA-111-SC-191151

Captured documents, reports from prisoners and other intercepted messages all contributed to von Schlieben's tale of woe.

General Collins' verbal orders for 24 June reinforced the plans outlined several days earlier. The Regiments on the flanks of the Corps, the 60th and the 22nd, would continue to confine German troops operating around Cap de la Hague and Maupertus airfield, while the rest of the Corps concentrated on breeching the ring of forts around Cherbourg. With the help of the Air Force and heavy artillery concentrations, 9th Division would seize the hills southwest of the city, while 79th Division's cleared la Mare à Canards south of the port. Now that 4th Division had finally shaken itself free from Bois du Rondou and Bois de Coudray, it was ready to advance onto the high ground overlooking Tourlaville.

9th Division

39th Regiment had moved up on the Division's right flank overnight and 2nd Battalion's first task was to clear the remaining entrenchments around Le Saussy. Company E captured the anti-aircraft position on the summit of Hill 151 at an early stage but it was forced to retire when a supporting artillery battalion began shelling the position. It was an unfortunate misunderstanding. Before long the German crews had returned and turned their guns on 2nd Battalion. Company F's commander requested permission to retake Hill 151 but he was assured that 47th Regiment was about to attack the summit.

3rd Battalion had been advancing on the Regiment's right flank, making progress under heavy fire along the wooded slopes overlooking the Divette stream. Engineers were supposed to repair a bridge over the stream to allow Lieutenant-Colonel Stumpf to cross but it was evident that the Germans were intent on holding the far bank. Colonel Flint ordered Stumpf to withdraw from the stream and join the rest of the Regiment on the summit of Hill 171. The move brought Stumpf's men into contact with some hidden machine gun posts on the edge of Bois du Mont du Roc and Company I found itself under heavy fire. The German positions were too close to shell with artillery so Stumpf called up his armoured support and as the infantry fanned out to locate the enemy posts, tank-destroyers moved into position, destroying the machine guns

Two rifle grenadiers of 39th Regiment creep up on a German strongpoint; note the 'AAA' insignia on their helmets. NARA-111-SC-190795-S

one by one. Company I searched the undergrowth after the firing stopped and discovered that naval and service personnel had manned the machine guns. The rest of the woods were found to be clear of enemy troops and although the attack on Hill 151 had been stopped, Colonel Flint was pleased to report that Bois du Mont du Roc had been taken.

In 47th Regiment's sector, 2nd Battalion was making good progress, finding an abandoned headquarters and barracks complex to the west of Nouainville. However, Major Schmidt's advance came to an abrupt halt when anti-aircraft guns positioned on the walls of Fort Neuf, spotted his leading company. The battalion was in an exposed position, silhouetted on the skyline and although tank-destroyers were available, a second strongpoint near Hainneville opened fire as they moved forward: '2nd Battalion is advancing and getting a hell of a lot of direct fire on left flank.'

After helping to clear Bois du Mont du Roc, 3rd Battalion waited for orders to advance onto Hill 151 and while a misunderstanding with the artillery was cleared up, snipers began to infiltrate Clayman's assembly area: '3rd Bn CO desires to know when the start will be made, having a battle in its CP [command post] right now.'

The artillery barrage failed to silence the position on the summit of the hill and Clayman's men were stopped in their tracks by the deadly anti-aircraft guns.

While 47th Regiment and 39th Regiment struggled to advance onto Hill 151, 60th Regiment was preparing to clear the high ground north and west of Flottemanville-Hague. 3rd Battalion continued to watch the roads leading towards Cap de la Hague peninsula as the rest of the Regiment waited for their supporting barrage to begin. In the meantime, the Germans had been preparing their own attack and at first light Colonel Rohan was alarmed to hear that Lieutenant-Colonel Kauffman was calling for assistance to deal with a threat to his position:

> 'A field right across our front is full of Germans, We are putting fire on it and want a Cub plane to observe for us, for artillery fire.'

Company I moved forward to reinforce Hill 180 as the rest of the battalion prepared for action. They faced a long wait. The German attack failed to materialise and after several hours of inactivity Kauffman requested assistance from the Reconnaissance Troop: 'Believes Jerry in front of them wants to give up and are ripe for propaganda.'

Rather than moving forward to attack, the German soldiers were looking to surrender and following negotiations, 1st Battalion sent their prisoners to the rear.

The need to advance appeared to have disappeared but as Colonel Rohan ordered his men to hold their positions, General Eddy had other plans. Strongpoint 19 was directing fire onto 47th Regiment's flank and Rohan was ordered to clear it to break the deadlock.

Throughout the morning tanks had been seen and heard moving around the strongpoint and Colonel Rohan made sure 3rd Battalion had plenty of its own armour before it advanced. While the tanks of Company B, 746th Tank Battalion moved forward towards Strongpoint 19, their commanding officer found himself in an unusual predicament:

> 'At about 13:00 twenty friendly aircraft strafed the CP killing several of the American soldiers. At that particular time Captain Pay was at the regimental aid station having his foot treated. He had been having trouble with an infected foot for the past week or so. All the aid men as well as all the personnel hit their foxholes when the attack came. Captain Pay was left stranded in the open with his sore foot in a bucket of water. He survived the attack unharmed however.'

a way across a stream and an anti-tank ditch. The final approach to the fort, a narrow promontory, had been cleared of trees and undergrowth, creating a killing zone for the pillboxes and mortar pits beyond. Fort du Roule was a perfect example of defensive engineering and it would test Colonel Robinson's men to the limit.

3rd Battalion ran into heavy fire from Point 44 as it advanced into the valley. Machine guns and 88s on the far side of the stream stopped Company I in its tracks, wounding Captain Petras as he led his men forward for a third time. Anti-aircraft positions on the Octeville heights had a perfect view of 2nd Battalion's advance and enfilade fire forced Lieutenant-Colonel Huff to abandon his attempt to cross the stream; air and artillery support would be needed before 314th Regiment could reach Fort du Roule.

As 313th Regiment approached the heights overlooking Hau Gringor quarry, 2nd and 3rd Battalion spotted dozens of German artillerymen abandoning their guns and running for cover. Some turned to fire on Wood's men as they struggled to find a way through belts of barbed wire protecting the artillery positions and brought the advance to a halt. While the Regiment regrouped, patrols investigated the cliff top finding a large number of artillery emplacements; 313th Regiment would eventually find two 170mm guns, three 155mm howitzers, several smaller guns and a huge stockpile of ammunition. 3rd Battalion led the advance into Hau Gringor village later that evening, driving the German artillerymen before them. The GIs showed no mercy and in the words of the Regimental Diary the rout 'afforded excellent shooting for the BARs', 320 prisoners were eventually rounded up in the nearby quarry.

4th Division

Following 12th Regiment's overnight push towards Tourlaville, 8th Regiment had fallen behind as it struggled to drive *Kampfgruppen* Koehn from the high ground overlooking the Trottebec valley. The Air Force paved the way and as zero hour approached Colonel van Fleet's men marked the two German strongpoints with purple smoke.

2nd Battalion had taken over from the shattered 3rd Battalion in front of Strongpoint 190190 (named after its map reference) and once the fighter-bombers had flown over, Lieutenant-

111

GIs clear and occupy a German anti-aircraft gun position.

Colonel MacNeely's men crawled as towards their objective while 29th Field Artillery Battalion shelled the strongpoint. The artillery was firing only six rounds a minute to minimise the chance of 'friendly' casualties but as Company E drew closer, Lieutenant Rebarchek was concerned that the shells were falling too close to his men. The artillery observer ordered his guns to lift their range for the final salvo; it proved to be a fatal error. The gunners misjudged their range and the smoke shells intended to cover as Company E's assault, exploded beyond the target. There was no time to rearrange the barrage; Rebarchek's men would have to take their chances:

'Company E, with bayonets fixed, advanced through the orchards and over the next hedgerow where they received terrific fire from the enemy positions. 1st Platoon reached a small hedge just short of the line of barbed wire, and from this position silenced a 40mm gun that was in a concrete pit at the road fork, but they were unable to advance any further. 3rd Platoon on the right, stopped by fire from the front, was ordered to move farther to the right behind a second hedgerow. They passed through

*another orchard and entered a wheat-field beyond the hedgerow
behind which they intended to advance.'*

3rd Platoon faced six machine guns and when 2nd Platoon tried to outflank the position, the Germans were waiting for them: 'The Krauts came up and threw everything but their shoes at Company E.'

As casualties mounted, Rebarchek crawled back to the mortar platoon and radioed Battalion Headquarters for armoured support. Lieutenant-Colonel MacNeely informed him that Company B, 70th Tank Battalion, was still operating with the 1st Battalion; Rebarchek would have to try and hold on until they arrived.

Meanwhile, the fighter-bombers had paved the way for a surprising success on 1st Battalion's front:

*'At 11:00 twelve P47s dropped twenty-four 1,000lb bombs on
the strongpoint in front of 1st Battalion; twenty-three bombs hit
the target. Immediately the enemy troops came out of the
fortification and started running across the fields, where they
were slaughtered by mortar fire. The strongpoint, which had
been a tough nut the previous day, was taken without further
trouble.'*

1st Battalion overran the position in record time allowing Company B, 70th Tank Battalion, to withdraw and move to support 2nd Battalion.

Company E held out for three hours in front of Strongpoint 190190, suffering grievous casualties as they waited for the Shermans to arrive. Eventually, Rebarchek conceded defeat and decided to pull his men his men back and regroup:

*'About 14:00 Lieutenant Rebarchek decided that his
company was being pounded to pieces for no purpose and since
he had received no answer to his request, he withdrew his troops
behind the hedgerow 200 yards south of the road fork. Here they
were still under heavy fire from the front and right flank. 88s, a
battery of 100mms and several 20mms were still firing at them
from 200 or 300 yards, in addition to mortars, machine guns and
rifles.'*

Only forty made it back.

When the Shermans eventually located Company E, the tank commander refused to get out of his tank into the hail of bullets. In frustration Rebarchek climbed onto the platoon leader's tank and shouted directions through the open hatch. With Rebarchek hanging from the turret of their platoon leaders tank, the Shermans started to move followed closely by the depleted Company E. As the tanks crawled towards Strongpoint 190190 they found that Germans were waiting for them:

'As soon as the tanks came into view, the 88's opened up on them. One tank had its track knocked off and the others stopped. It was some time before Lieutenant Rebarchek could get them to move forward again, but when they did they broke the enemy position. One tank came up on the left of the 88 at the house, whereupon nine Germans at that position and at the road fork put up white flags. Two tanks on the right swung behind the hedgerow on the enemy left flank; the Germans then fled north to the road, and then marched down towards Company B in columns of twos, all carrying white flags.'

Forty men surrendered to Company B, leaving behind a huge arsenal of weapons and ammunition. When 2nd Battalion searched the position, they found four 100mm artillery pieces, four 88s, one 40mm and five 20mm AA guns, mortars, machine guns and over 200 rifles.

While 2nd Battalion cleared Strongpoint 190190, the Germans had counterattacked 1st Battalion's as it regrouped. Lieutenant-Colonel Simmonds was arranging artillery support when

Soldiers take a well-earned rest having cleared a German strongpoint.
NARA-111-SC-190979

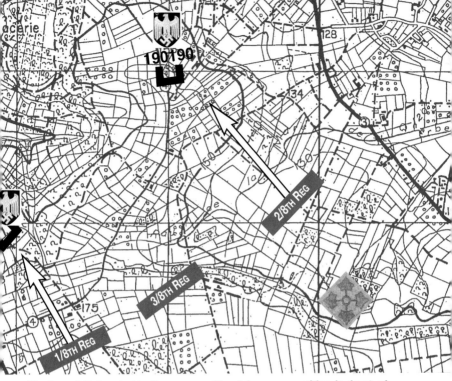

Lieutenant Rebarchek's Company suffered heavy casualties in front of Strongpoint 190190

disaster struck; a shell exploded in the centre of 1st Battalion's headquarters (a line of foxholes dug into an embankment), killing Simmonds' and wounding several staff. As a junior officer tried in vain to convince the artillery that he was in desperate need of support, Major-General Barton arrived on the scene. With no time for formalities, the General grabbed the phone and shouted down the receiver; '... this is Barton, I want all the artillery I've got to fire on ...' and gave the coordinates. The surprised radio operator responded immediately and minutes later a deluge of shells scattered the German attack.

The fighting on 8th Regiment's front began to die down as the light faded and as the Germans melted away into the wooded Trottebec valley, 3rd Battalion surrounded a number of entrenchments. It looked as though the Germans would surrender without a fight but as G Company commanding officer persuaded the German officers to lay down their arms an unfortunate incident occurred:

'Captain Wilson was negotiating with German officers for surrender, when someone in G Company fired. Germans cut

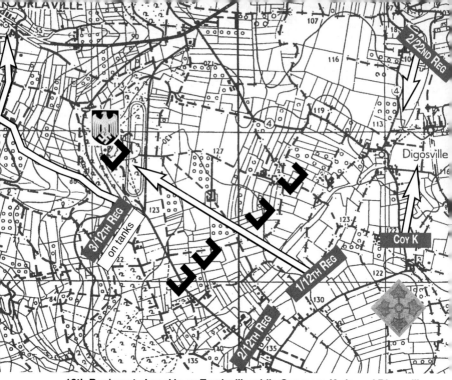

12th Regiment closed in on Tourlaville while Company K cleared Digosville to the rear.

down, and killed Captain Wilson and wounded several men.'

On 12th Regiment's front Colonel van Fleet was hoping to clear the high ground overlooking Tourlaville. Undercover of darkness 1st Battalion forded a stream across their front, followed by six Sherman tanks, and moved as close as they dare to a line of German strongpoints southwest of Digosville. Fighter-bombers flew over at sunrise and although several overshot their target, dropping their bombs on 1st Battalion's position, the aerial bombardment shattered the Germans' morale. The strongpoints were quickly overrun and 225 prisoners were taken, many of them coastal artillerymen and naval personnel. As the battalion regrouped, the headquarters company came under fire from a farmhouse. A group of determined fanatics had let the infantry and tanks bypass their position, preferring to strike at the soft vehicles of the rear echelon unit. Three machine guns had pinned down Major Johnson's staff and they threatened to disrupt 12th Regiment's advance on Tourlaville. Two tanks were recalled to convince the Germans to surrender, but after they refused Johnson decided to force the issue. Two prisoners accompanied the tanks as they moved towards the farmhouse and although the Germans inside held their fire, they still refused to surrender. As the Shermans pulled up in the farmyard their 75mm guns opened fire, reducing the building to a smouldering ruin. Thirty-five men ran from the rubble; they were all gunned down by the tanks' machine guns. As 1st Battalion regrouped, 2nd Battalion took over the advance and by nightfall it had secured its objective, a complex of bunkers on the final ridge overlooking Cherbourg.

While the rest of the Regiment moved towards Tourlaville, 3rd Battalion supported 22nd Regiment as it attacked Digosville and despite poor coordination between the two Regiments, the infantry worked its way forward covered by four Sherman tanks. Twelve P47s paved the way for Company K's final assault, and once again the air strike broke the Germans' morale. Many fled towards Maupertus airfield but by dusk Lieutenant-Colonel Merrill's men had rounded up 150 prisoners and six artillery pieces.

For the second day in a row, Colonel Luckett decided to send troops forward under cover of darkness but as 3rd Battalion

A Sherman tank makes its way past two knocked out Panzer IVs.
NARA-111-SC-191371

moved forward to rendezvous with Company A, 70th Tank Battalion, disaster struck. As scouts escorted Lieutenant-Colonel Merrill and two of his officers forward, a Sherman accidently fired on the group killing Merrill and seven of his men. It was the second time the battalion had lost its CO in as many days.

Nine Shermans, with half a dozen men clinging to their turrets, led the advance into the village of Tourlaville while the rest of the battalion marched alongside. *Kampfgruppen* Koehn had already withdrawn into the city of Cherbourg and by midnight 3rd Battalion had taken the western end of the village. Colonel Luckett's plan to penetrate deep into the enemy lines had succeeded; 12th Regiment was in a position to advance into the city alongside 79th Division. As it began to grow light the GIs in Tourlaville waited expectantly for the Germans to retaliate. The attack never came; the only German troops in sight were medics searching the hillside above the village for wounded. The road into Cherbourg lay open.

Fires burn out of control as German engineers destroy the port's facilities.
NARA-111-SC-191030

CHAPTER NINE

25 June – Overlooking the port

As General Collins made his plans for the final assault on Cherbourg, thousands of GIs tried to rest in their foxholes on hills surrounding the port. Lee MacCardell, correspondent for the *Baltimore Sun*, came across one group of soldiers as they dug in for the night:

'The Joes looked like they could stand a Saturday night bath anywhere, those with beards looked like burlesque tramps. All were beginning to tire a little. Many a Joe hadn't taken his shoes off for a week, his feet were killing him. He would have given ten bucks for a pair of ten-cent socks. Aside from canned rations and hand grenades, which filled all the pockets of his grimy, mud-stained fatigues, he carried only what he wore plus his canteen, a shovel, an ammunition belt, an extra bandolier, a knife, a bayonet and his rifle.'

Weary GIs make coffee in the outskirts of Cherbourg. NARA-111-SC-190794-S

Two Russians who had been forced to work for the Germans slip through the lines to meet up with the American troops. NARA-111-SC-190748

All three of VII Corps' divisions were poised on the heights overlooking Cherbourg and General Collins had arranged with the Air Force to drop propaganda leaflets offering surrender terms:

> *'Those who will surrender will not be harmed. Throw down your arms. Come out waving leaflets or some other white object.'*

It was known that many of the troops guarding the city were Eastern Europeans with dubious morale and Collins was hoping to entice some of them to give themselves up.

At first light the Adjutant of Cherbourg's Naval Hospital approached a patrol of the 9th Division accompanied by a captured American Air Force officer. The pair were escorted to General Eddy's headquarters and asked him to spare the hospital from shelling. Plasma was handed over to help care for wounded American soldiers in the Adjutant's care and he was also given an ultimatum to pass on to General von Schlieben:

'The Fortress Cherbourg is now surrounded and its defences have been breached. The city is now isolated. ... You are tremendously outnumbered and it is merely a question of time when Cherbourg must be captured. The immediate unconditional surrender of Cherbourg is demanded....'

General Bradley had arranged naval support for the final assault on the city and a task force of three battleships, four cruisers and a number of destroyers had moved into position on 24 June. The ships waited until VII Corps confirmed its troop dispositions but the first attempt to provide support for the ground troops ended in failure. As the task force sailed close to the coastline, German shore batteries opened fire with deadly accuracy, straddling several ships with their salvoes. The Naval Commander took immediate evasive action and switched his guns to counter battery fire as his ships turned out of range. *Festung* Cherbourg had proved that it was still capable of repulsing an attack from the sea; the only consolation was that 9th Division had been able to locate several enemy batteries in the Cap de la Hague area.

9th Division

On 60th Regiment's front, flares and the sounds of digging raised concerns that *Kampfgruppen* Mueller was preparing to counterattack from the direction of Ste Croix-Hague. Patrols were fired on as they investigated and Major Houston's patrol came across a 'Goliath', a two metre long remote controlled mine. After reporting the device to the engineers the GIs

Engineers disarm Goliaths, remote controlled explosive devices.
NARA-111-SC-190621

continued on their way; a few minutes later the 'Goliath' exploded leaving a fifteen metre wide crater.

Colonel Rohan's main objective was to prevent German troops retaking captured positions and roadblocks supported by anti-tank guns and light tanks were posted on every road and track. Patrols completed the cordon and Rohan warned his battalion commanders to keep their men on the move: '... you get just as many casualties sitting still as you do moving.'

3rd Battalion investigated a strongpoint close to Tonneville during the afternoon but when Company I came under heavy fire, Colonel Rohan withdrew his troops and called on the Navy for assistance. The combination of shells from warships and the divisional artillery subdued the position. Patrols later reported that Tonneville was in ruins and the local population believed that the German soldiers had fled towards Cap de la Hague.

47th Regiment objective for 25 June was to clear three Napoleonic fortresses overlooking the outskirts of Cherbourg. 3rd Battalion faced Redoubte des Fourches, a huge fortification protected by barbed wire and rooftop pillboxes. A short artillery

The spoils of war; GIs display a Nazi flag they have just found.
NARA-111-SC-191014

ANSE STE. — ANNE

L. W. M.

Fort de Couplets

EQUEURDREVILLE

247TH REGIMENT

Haut du Tot

Hameau du Tot

Redoubte des Fourches

3/47TH REGIMENT

47th Regiment attacked the Napoleonic forts to the west of Cherbourg.

123

Coastal batteries dug into the cliffs protected Cherbourg from an amphibious assault. NARA-111-SC-190509-S

bombardment paved the way for Lieutenant-Colonel Clayman's attack and as shells slammed into the fort, the ammunition dump exploded into flames. White flags had already begun to appear on the roof of the fort by the time 3rd Battalion advanced and although a few shots were fired, the garrison soon surrendered. Redoute des Fourches burned out of control as the prisoners emerged and the exploding ammunition made it too dangerous to take tanks past the fort. 3rd Battalion would have to wait until the fires had died down.

2nd Battalion faced Fort de Couplets, standing high on an isolated hill protected by a dry moat and barbed wire. A squadron of P-47's bombed the fort to begin with, and as the artillery and mortars shelled the hilltop position, tank-destroyers blasted paths through the wire entanglements. The preparatory bombardment shattered the German morale and white flags appeared on the walls of the fort as Company E started to climb the slopes. Fifteen minutes after the assault started eighty-nine men surrendered. Company F had also cleared the fort at Hameau du Tot and had found abandoned artillery pieces and huge piles of munitions in the village of

Equeurdreville to the northeast.

39th Regiment had spent the night patrolling the outskirts of Octeville and even though members of the French underground had questioned the local population, only one patrol reported meeting the enemy:

> 'Started talking to them before they were sure they were Germans, our patrol fired several shots and Jerry took off. All houses along the route were empty, no pillboxes, trenches or roadblocks were found.'

The situation on Colonel Flint's front was vague but as soon as 39th Regiment advanced 3rd Battalion came under fire from across the Divette valley as it crossed the Octeville heights. Lieutenant-Colonel Stumpf had to wait for artillery support before he could resume the advance towards Octeville. Meanwhile, 2nd Battalion pushed quickly into Octeville the village, capturing a group of soldiers guarding an ammunition dump. One prisoner reported that there were 'no heavy weapons, just machine guns, wire and steel obstacles' in front of the battalion but as soon as Lieutenant-Colonel Gunn's men began the descent into the city, rooftop anti-aircraft guns opened

Artillery observers look on as their guns shell the city of Cherbourg.
NARA-111-SC-190859

fire. The 20mm flak canons wreaked havoc as they fired indiscriminately up the hill and although a German tank had been spotted lurking around the city cemetery, Colonel Flint had ruled out armoured support for Gunn's men. Many of the AA guns were stationed close to the Maritime Hospital and there was a danger of hitting the building. Clouds of smoke and dust drifting over the city were making it difficult for artillery observer on Fort Neuf to identify targets. Fearing heavy casualties, Colonel Flint ordered Lieutenant-Colonel Gunn to hold his position until the 3rd Battalion had been able to move up.

While 39th Regiment reorganised in Octeville, 47th Regiment was ordered to cut the coast road to prevent German soldiers leaving the city and while Company E moved towards the beach, the rest of 2nd Battalion headed towards the Arsenal. 88mm guns, mortars and *Nebelwerfers* covered the German infantry as they made a careful withdrawal towards Rue Gambetta. Progress was slow but Colonel Smythe's men worked their way forward clearing block after block of snipers and anti-tank guns. The battalion's 81mm mortars scored an important success when the infantry spotted a number of *Nebelwerfers* on the city's cycle track; a short barrage destroyed seven of the deadly weapons.

The rest of the Regiment headed into the city in the face of heavy fire from rooftop 20mm anti-aircraft guns. The infantry crept forward from doorway to doorway locating pillboxes, calling forward the armour once an enemy position had been located. A pillbox in front of the Naval College stopped 1st Battalion's advance and it took 15th Combat Engineer Battalion bulldozers several hours to carve a route through the rubble for the tank-destroyers. General Eddy encouraged Colonel Smythe to 'keep plugging' but a second bunker covering the Maritime hospital refused to surrender, enduring dozens of direct hits from the tank-destroyers. After two hours Lieutenant-Colonel Clayman conceded defeat and withdrew his men to a safe distance. The artillery would have to 'bust it open'.

As it began to grow dark cracks began to show in the Germans' morale, 47th Regiment had already taken hundreds of prisoners, clearing large parts of the city suburbs:

'Determined resistance was met along all the way and the fighting was fierce for every yard gained... Slow going, fighting

A Sherman tank rolls through the ruins looking for snipers. NARA-111-SC-191085

all the way, Germans appear to be letting up, a lot of prisoners.'
39th Regiment's failure to push beyond Octeville left Colonel
Smythe's right flank exposed and General Eddy gave the order
to withdraw, the two Regiments would complete the task in the
morning.

79th Division

313th Regiment's patrols had managed to penetrate the
suburbs during the night and had found few signs of organised
resistance; the German troops had either fled or surrendered as

Fort du Roule, Pillboxes line the wall of the Napoleonic fortress.
NARA-111-SC-200571

While 39th Regiment cleared the Octeville Heights, 314th Regiment struggled to advance towards Fort du Roule.

P47 Thunderbolt.

Colonel Wood's men approached. The patrols withdrew at first light as the guns in the lower levels of Fort du Roule came to life once more. The fort had to be taken before 313th Regiment could move into the city.

A squadron of P47s flying low overhead signalled the start of 314th Regiment's attack on Fort du Roule. The cliff top position was a prominent target but many of the planes still overshot their target and their bombs exploded harmlessly on the hillside. Artillery and mortars fired a covering barrage of high explosive and smoke shells at the fort as Colonel Robinson's men moved into the valley. German infantry emerged from a hidden trench and fired on 3rd Battalion as it began to climb towards the fort. With the artillery fully employed shelling the summit of the hill, Colonel Robinson ordered 2nd and 3rd Battalions' support weapons to open fire on the position. The combined firepower of the machine gun and mortar platoons forced the Germans to retire. Only a handful escaped, the rest were cut down as they ran. 3rd Battalion quickly occupied the trench and dug in to wait for the 2nd Battalion.

2nd Battalion's advance had stalled in the face of heavy machine gun fire and as the two leading companies tried to reach Point 44, mortars and artillery on the Octeville heights began shelling their positions. For two hours Lieutenant-Colonel Huff's men endured the barrage of shells and bullets as they regrouped for a second attack. This time 3rd Battalion was able to provide covering fire and once Company F had reached

314th Regiment faced pillboxes and barbed wire as it climbed the promontory to reach Fort du Roule.

Point 44 the machine gun fire abated allowing the rest of the battalion to advance. After clearing a few of the bunkers (finding a large stock of champagne and cognac in one) 2nd Battalion pushed onto the ridge, leaving 1st Battalion to deal with the rest.

Company F headed towards Point 46, a heavily defended anti-aircraft position on top of the cliff, while the rest of the battalion advanced towards Fort du Roule, codenamed Point 45. 3rd Battalion gave covering fire as Company G worked their way along the southern face of the promontory, clearing a number of outlying bunkers. Company E headed straight for the fort, and once they had crossed a deep anti-tank ditch, Lieutenant-Colonel Huff's men faced a maze of barbed wire and pillboxes. At first the situation looked promising as a white flag appeared above one bunker. Major Miller encouraged the men inside to surrender but as soon as they emerged with their hands up, a nearby pillbox opened fire cutting them down. It proved that many soldiers holding the bunkers protecting Fort du Roule were willing to fight to the last man.

As Company E crawled forward one platoon was caught in a

hail of machine gun bullets, killing and wounding several men. The survivors struggled to find cover on the bare slope and as casualties mounted, Corporal John D Kelly volunteered to go forward alone and knock out the bunker:

> *'Arming himself with a pole charge about ten feet long, with fifteen pounds of TNT affixed, he climbed the slope under a withering blast of machine-gun fire and placed the charge at the strongpoint's base. The subsequent blast was ineffective, and again, alone and unhesitatingly, he braved the slope to repeat the operation. This second blast blew off the ends of the enemy guns. Corporal Kelly then climbed the slope a third time to place a pole charge at the strongpoint's rear entrance. When this had been blown open he hurled hand grenades inside the position forcing survivors of the enemy gun crews to come out and surrender.'*

Corporal (later Sergeant) Kelly's actions helped the rest of Company E work their way forward towards Fort du Roule. He was recommended for the Congressional Medal of Honor but it was awarded posthumously as he was mortally wounded five months later.

Satchel charges and grenades blasted the bunkers throughout

Soldiers look on as engineers try to silence the guns on the cliff face while the port burns in the distance. NARA-111-SC-200570

the morning and by midday Lieutenant-Colonel Huff's men were closing in on the fort's courtyard, having taken over 500 German soldiers prisoner. The garrison of the main building refused to surrender and made use of the huge stocks of ammunition and supplies in the lower levels of the fort. Company E kept inching forward and by 15:00 Colonel Robinson was pleased to hear that the courtyard had been taken. Men had also broken into the fort and cleared the top level but still the men on the floors below refused to surrender: 'Situation unchanged. Very little fire from sealed positions, 2nd Battalion bringing in 250 prisoners.'

Once the cliff top had been secured, 3rd Battalion advanced into the Divette valley, a narrow pass flanked by the Octeville heights and Fort du Roule. Company K was immediately pinned down by machine guns protecting a 88mm AA position high on the slopes. The recently promoted company commander, 1st Lieutenant Carlos C Ogden, refused to let his men be cut to pieces and climbed towards the enemy position armed with a rifle, hand grenades and rifle grenades. Despite being wounded twice, he destroyed the flak gun with a rifle grenade before eliminating two machine gun nests with hand grenades. His bravery allowed Company K to resume its advance. Lieutenant Ogden was later awarded the Congressional Medal of Honor for his part in the capture of the Fort du Roule.

Down in the valley below, Company L had charged across an open field to reach a pillbox, throwing grenades and satchel charges through the firing slits. The men inside refused to surrender and held Company L at bay until nightfall.

While the rest of 314th Regiment made slow progress towards and past Fort du Roule, Company F had spent the last six hours pinned down in front of Point 46 east of the fort. The first sign that the men on the cliff top wished to surrender was seen at dusk. However, as the GIs edged forward it became clear that some men wanted to fight on:

'Fortification 46 showing white flag but as our troops advance to take prisoners, they come under fire from 88mm gun.'

Ninety men eventually surrendered an hour later when they ran out of ammunition.

Even though the top floor of Fort du Roule had been taken, the rest of the garrison refused to surrender. Attempts to

General Collins surveys the city from the roof of Fort du Roule.

negotiate failed and while some of Colonel Huff's men tried to break down the doors with explosives, others tossed grenades and satchel charges down the cliff face to try and damage the guns below. AA guns on Octeville heights across the valley prevented volunteers from climbing onto the cliff face to reach the embrasures at the base of the fort. Engineers temporarily silenced the guns by dangling pole charges down the cliff on pieces of wire and detonating them with a makeshift triggers.

With the menace from Fort du Roule finished, General Wyche decided it was time to explore Cherbourg and as it began to grow dark 313th Regiment made its way down the hill into the suburbs with the following orders:

'Do not stop, do not loot, strong security on flanks. Take prisoners, Cannon Company fires to be lifted on flares... Not much fighting expected. If we do fight, get AT guns into action, do not waste men.'

The advance was unopposed and by nightfall Colonel Wood's men had occupied the southeast corner of the city. It meant that

133

The advance into Cherbourg begins. NARA-111-SC-190809-S

313th Regiment was ready to push deep into the heart of the port in the morning.

4th Division

As 4th Division closed in on Cherbourg, General Barton withdrew 8th Regiment from the line so it could concentrate on clearing the Trottebec valley. Meanwhile, 22nd Regiment had increased its grip on the high ground east of the city, rounding up hundreds of prisoners around Bretteville and on the coast north of Hill 158. 12th Regiment would make the final push into the eastern suburbs of the city.

Colonel Luckett's 3rd Battalion was already firmly established in Tourlaville, following its daring drive the previous night. The rest of the Regiment needed to advance towards the sea, clearing the ridge overlooking the village and seize a coastal battery before it could enter the port. Fighter-bombers paved the way and as Major Johnson went ahead to assess the garrison's reaction he was relieved to see white flags flying above the casemates. He could also see that while the direct route to the battery was too exposed, a wooded ravine offered a sheltered approach. The tanks waited at a safe distance, and 1st Battalion moved forward:

> 'From a distance two white flags could be seen above the fort. As the leading companies entered a wooded draw just in front of the objective they were fired on from the fort by mortars and 20mm, and six men were wounded. The white flags still waved over the fort.'

The six wounded men were all part of Major Johnson's command group and for the second time in the campaign the battalion was left without a staff and no means of contacting its artillery. Tanks would have to be used.

After reorganising his men, Johnson personally guided the Shermans to the rear of the battery and while they repeatedly fired their 75mm guns at the bunkers, the GIs worked their way through the complex. A German major waving a white flag marked the capitulation of the battery and while Major Johnson

12th Regiment closes in on the eastern suburbs of Cherbourg.

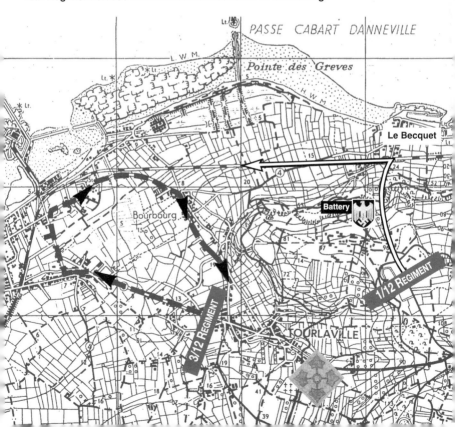

negotiated with his opposite number his men completed their search. Three casemated eight-inch guns looking out to sea formed the backbone of the fort. 88mm and 20mm anti-aircraft guns protected the battery from air and ground attack. Johnson's men also discovered an officers' club and a hospital crammed with wounded men. Major Johnson allowed the German medical officer to stay with his patients, but the rest were evacuated immediately. 1st Battalion had captured over 400 men and an important position covering the eastern approaches to Cherbourg.

1st Battalion's next objective was le Becquet on the coast and as the GIs made their way down the steep cliffs into the village, a civilian pointed out a 20mm AA gun on the seawall. A white flag marked the position but as Johnson watched through his binoculars it disappeared from view. A similar treachery had earlier wiped out his staff and this time Johnson was taking no chances. Lieutenant Esschbacher, the Cannon Company liaison officer radioed the coordinates of the AA position through to his howitzers. A few minutes later the German position was silenced. As 1st Battalion entered le Becquet the local population lined the main street and showered the GIs with flowers as they marched past. Fort Ile de Pelée, one of the Napoleonic forts on the harbour's breakwater, opened fire as 1st Battalion advanced along the coast towards Cherbourg; the divisional artillery quickly silenced the guns.

Once 1st Battalion had cleared the coastal battery on the ridge overlooking Tourlaville, 3rd Battalion had started to explore the roads to Cherbourg. Company I was only supposed to patrol a short distance into the city before turning towards Bourbourg on the coast. However, the company commander missed the road junction he required and led his men over a mile into the Marais district of the city before noticing the mistake. The error uncovered an interesting development. The Germans had evacuated the district, leaving the area in front of 12th Regiment clear of enemy troops. On hearing the news, General Collins ordered General Barton to move quickly. VII Corps' commanding officer watched the final phase of the battle from the hills southeast of the city:

'Off to the left were the steep cliffs of the highlands that run right up to the back door of the city. Another of our divisions was rapidly closing in on this area from the south and we could see

The local population turn out to greet their liberators. NARA-111-SC-190414-S

smoke from the fires being directed into Fort du Roule. Over to the right were the inner and outer breakwaters with the old French forts guarding the entrance from the sea. Beyond the haze of smoke we could see part of our battle fleet engaging in shelling the seacoast batteries west of the town. Within this flame, the city lay in a bowl from which billows of smoke poured up in the places where the Germans were destroying stores of oil and ammunition. As we watched one of our heavy batteries fired a perfect concentration onto a German position just west of Fort des Flamands. It was a thrilling and in a sense, awe-inspiring sight. I knew that Cherbourg was ours and directed Tubby [General Barton's nickname] *to push one of his Regiment's into the eastern section of the city before that night.'*

As Colonel Luckett looked out across the burning city from a

German bunker above Tourlaville, he was joined by Major-General Barton and General Roosevelt. Barton was confident that 12th Regiment's attack had been meticulously planned and gave its commander his full support, 'It's your show Jim... Run it anyway you see fit... I'll back you one hundred percent of the way.'

Tanks blew holes in the German barricades and the engineers cleared mines from the along the railway while the infantry waited to advance. 2nd Battalion was first off the mark, moving quickly along Rue du General Leclerc into the Les Mielles area. Nebelwerfers retaliated, firing a barrage of oil-filled shells; the range was too far and the missiles exploded harmlessly behind the battalion. 3rd Battalion followed, working its way through the industrial area along Boulevard Maritime. Company K's advance came to a halt as it crossed Rue Etienne Dolet; pillboxes on the Quai du Normandie had a clear view of the quayside and the company commander redirected his men to follow Company I along Rue Carnot.

The two battalions cleared their objectives in record time and,

General Wyche's permission pushed on into 79th Division's area, reaching Rue de la Bretonnière. 1st Battalion's came under fire as it crossed Rue Carnot en route to Fort des Flamands, the Napoleonic fort protecting the eastern approaches to the port. The French Resistance had warned Colonel Luckett about a number of pillboxes along the seafront and the information had been confirmed by an unexpected source:

> '1st Battalion was assisted by a woman member of the British espionage, who gave detailed descriptions of the fortifications which were the objective of the battalion. She warned that the attack should not be attempted with infantry alone, since the Germans in concrete dugouts were twelve metres underground.'

It was too dark to deploy tanks and while Major Johnson organised his men, 155mm howitzers fired a supporting barrage, each gun firing one round per minute:

> 'The first artillery concentration fell at 23:24, exactly on the

4th Division advances to the sea front.

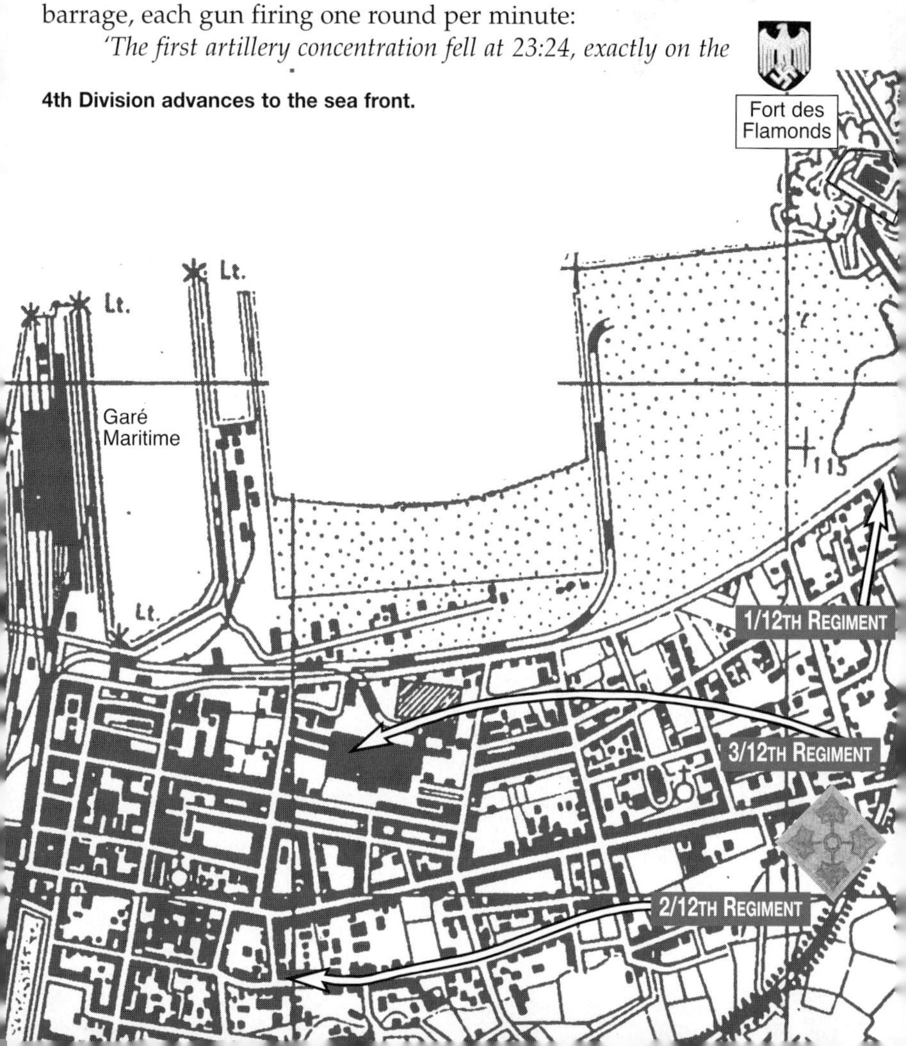

Fort des
Flamonds

Lt.

Lt.

Lt.

Garé
Maritime

Lt.

1/12TH REGIMENT

3/12TH REGIMENT

2/12TH REGIMENT

The walls of Fort des Flamands. NARA-111-SC-191047

Fort des Flamands from the inside, showing the devastating effect caused by bombing and shelling.

designated line, one block in front of the troops, and blew up an ammunition dump. The second concentration moved forward 100 yards and the third one hundred yards further, setting fire to buildings in the area. The final concentration was delivered at 23:34 and at 23:40.'

Guarding a silenced pillbox on the quayside.
NARA-111-SC-191004-S

The bombardment was devastating. Buildings burst into flames and collapsed in heaps of rubble while Company C followed as close as it dare. Some men reached the bunkers and, while others gave covering fire, pushed pole charges through the firing slits. The men inside showed no signs of surrendering and as casualties began to mount, Major Johnson ordered his men to regroup. The Germans had other ideas. As Company C crawled back to safety, dragging their wounded with them, flares were fired, illuminating the area. The battle raged throughout the night as 1st Battalion fought to rescue their men trapped around the bunkers, but the deadlock was only broken when tanks

German engineers had demolished large parts of the port before they surrendered. NARA-111-SC-191503

arrived at first light. As Major Johnson positioned the Shermans ready for a final assault, white flags started to appear; 350 soldiers eventually filed out of the pillboxes.

As VII Corps worked its way into the streets of Cherbourg, German engineers continued to systematically destroy the port facilities and throughout the night GIs watched as the city rocked with explosions:

'Cherbourg waterfront glows with the destruction of installations by the enemy. The Germans were busy destroying installations and it was difficult to tell at the time which explosions were their demolitions and which were our artillery fire. Early in the night Fort des Flamands went up in flames, followed a little later by the Amcot Aircraft works, the Gare Maritime, Fort de Chavagnac and other buildings.'

CHAPTER TEN

26 & 27 June – Clearing the city

9th Division

47th Regiment's first objective was to reoccupy the area cleared the previous day and Colonel Smythe had hoped to advance quickly towards the Naval Arsenal while his 2nd Battalion re-established road-blocks along the coast road. For the second time in three days there were difficulties with the artillery and a series of delays postponed zero hour. 1st Battalion decided not to wait for the barrage and C Company moved quickly and reached Rue Gambetta in front of the walls of the Arsenal two hours later:

The Arsenal, a huge fortification protecting Cherbourg's military port.

'Walls around Arsenal are 10 feet high and 30 feet thick... Embankment covered with wire, moat, earthen ramparts and high concrete walls with only three gates. Probably need grappling hooks and other scaling material... [Germans] have 20mm and 47mm there, covered by MGs.'

The rest of the battalion was heavily engaged around the Maritime Hospital and while Company A cleared the perimeter, Company B entered the buildings finding the wards crammed with wounded. As the two companies continued to push towards the Arsenal ambulances began to evacuate the building, finding 150 American soldiers amongst the 2,500 wounded men.

Gun positions guard the approaches to the Arsenal.

3rd Battalion waited impatiently for the artillery but when it started, two hours late, Lieutenant-Colonel Clayman was unimpressed: 'Believed it wasn't sufficient, but wanted to get it cleaned out.'

The battalion headed into St Sauveur accompanied by tank - destroyers and as one company engaged a strongpoint southwest of the Naval Hospital the other headed for the city cemetery where it captured the Headquarters Company of the 739th Infantry Regiment in an underground shelter. The commanding officer, Major Graefe, had wanted to surrender as soon as the American troops appeared but some of his men wanted to stage a final show of defiance. A few shots were fired at Clayman's troops but moments later Graefe and his men emerged with their hands up.

One by one Colonel Smythe's companies reached Rue Gambetta, finding the wide avenue covered by pillboxes and 20mm AA guns on the walls of the Arsenal. Tanks and tank-destroyers spent the afternoon cruising up and down Rue Gambetta but their armour piercing shells had no effect on the bunkers. 3rd Battalion eventually moved into position as it began to grow dark, having spent the afternoon engaging strongpoints around the Municipal Stadium. The Battalion's late arrival meant that General Eddy had postponed the attack on the Arsenal until the following morning and in the meantime public address systems were set up to broadcast news of General von Schlieben's surrender. There was still a glimmer of hope that *Generalmajor* Sattler might surrender the fortress without a fight.

39th Regiment made slow progress through Octeville and as 2nd Battalion cleared mines, the rooftop AA guns opened fire once again. 3rd Battalion also came under fire from the anti-

Sherman tanks patrol the ruins. NARA-111-SC-191166

Infantry search for snipers. NARA-111-SC-190974

146

aircraft guns across the Divette valley as it crossed the exposed Octeville heights. As 39th Regiment moved into the suburbs of St Sauveur, a new problem arose. The two battalions had failed to establish contact and as they advanced down the narrow streets reports of friendly fire began to increase.

After clearing up the confusion, the advance resumed and 2nd Battalion soon came across the small quarry where General von Schlieben's temporary headquarters was rumoured to be. A prisoner of war had earlier given information about the whereabouts of Cherbourg's Commandant and General Eddy had been pleased to pass on the news to his subordinate: 'Tell Colonel Flint that he will have the honour of capturing the German General.'

Another prisoner warned that the German staff had prepared an escape route; they would gather at the Prefect Maritime

before heading through the Arsenal to Fort Hainert where a boat was waiting to evacuate them to Cap de la Hague. The escape plan never materialised and at 15:40 Lieutenant-Colonel Gunn reported that his men were covering the entrance to the General's hideout:

'Am over the entrance to two tunnels which lead to subterranean. It is slow clearing up. Many reported underneath – shall soon know. It is questionable how many there are.'

A prisoner was sent down into the tunnels with an ultimatum to surrender but to begin with General von Schlieben refused to cooperate. Tank-destroyers moved in and after a few shots were fired, white flags were flown as dozens of German officers and orderlies began to emerge:

General von Schlieben.

'A few hours after the ultimatum was refused, Von Schlieben came out of a hole thirty feet underground and surrendered, while many of his troops fought on. With him were Rear Admiral Hennecke, second in command of Cherbourg, and 800 other officers and enlisted men.'

As Gunn's men began to round up the prisoners, British Commandos of 30 Assault Unit, Royal Marines, moved swiftly

Troops surround the entrance to von Schlieben's lair. NARA-111-SC-190804-S

into the tunnels searching for documents before the German staff could destroy them. Over the course of the next six days they would search several headquarters throughout the city finding useful intelligence material. The documents were returned to England and assessed by a team led by Commander Ian Fleming RNVR (the future author of the James Bond books).

General Collins and General Eddy came forward to meet General von Schlieben hoping to finalise the surrender of Cherbourg and prevent further loss of life. They were to be disappointed. The General refused to cooperate and pointed out that his communications system had broken down over twenty-four hours ago. When the means to communicate with the outlying forts was offered, von Schlieben again rejected the offer: 'The German General never did explain why he surrendered while his men continued to fight – or why he was not with them.'

Meanwhile, the two Regiments continued to push through the outskirts of Cherbourg, rounding up hundreds of prisoners as they neared the city centre. Hundreds of Germans (US 39th Regiment would take 2,100 prisoners by midnight) were willing to surrender and before long there was danger that General

148

GIs search von Schlieben's staff as they come to the surface.
NARA-111-SC-191084

Men of 314th Regiment round up prisoners from another underground headquarters. NARA-111-SC-190785-S

Bodies and debris litter the underground tunnels. NARA-111-SC-190797-S

Torpedoes line the walls of a subterranean fortress.
NARA-111-SC-190786-S

General Collins interviews General von Schlieben and Admiral Hennecke
NARA-111-SC-190786-S

313th Regiment hurry their prisoners into captivity.

Eddy's men could be overwhelmed. A shortage of transport made it difficult to evacuate the prisoners and the GIs resorted to cramming as many men onto the trucks as possible. Major Bradley noted that the record number of prisoners on a $2\frac{1}{2}$ tonne truck was seventy-six!

By nightfall 9th Division had cleared the western suburbs of Cherbourg and while patrols remained behind to enforce a curfew on the local population, General Eddy's men withdrew to prepare for the final attack on the Arsenal. Organised resistance had collapsed and during the night the Colonel in charge of the coastal defences surrendered 400 men to Lieutenant-Colonel Gunn when he learnt that General von Schlieben had been taken prisoner.

79th Division

General Wyche planned to send his men deep into the city at first light while Colonel Huff's continue to prise their way into Fort du Roule. Men of the 313th Regiment advanced steadily, and although a few fanatics continued to snipe from windows and rooftops, over 500 prisoners were taken in the first two hours. Sherman tanks followed close behind waiting for the infantry to call them forward to eliminate a strongpoint. McCardell, the correspondent for the *Baltimore Sun*, monitored the troops as they advanced through the ruins:

> 'We moved forward into a deserted quarter of the city, evidently a section in which working people had lived. Concussion had shattered every window, every hint of glass. The telephone and electric light wires were broken tangles. But most of the buildings did not appear to have been damaged seriously by either the bombings or the shellfire. The Germans had bricked up many windows and doors, leaving only narrow embrasures from which machine-guns would sweep the street.'

314th Regiment worked its way through the Val de Saire district and at times the Battalion commanders found it difficult to keep track of their companies. 3rd Battalion came under fire from Fort du Roule's flak guns as it cleared the Canal de Retenue area and Colonel Davis was angry that his men were not receiving the support they needed, 'Because of no communications he states that ack-ack are giving his battalion hell.'

A smoke screen provided by the Divisional artillery gave the necessary protection and by midday General Wyche was pleased to hear that both his Regiments were closing in on their objectives.

After 313th Regiment had finished clearing the inner

Heavy artillery move onto the quayside past the Tourist Information Office.
NARA-111-SC-190784-S

Aerial view of the ruined Gare Maritime. NARA-111-SC-199800

General Wyche's men were warned not to enter the station until it had been checked for booby-traps. NARA-111-SC-199799

harbour, 1st Battalion closed in on the railway sidings only to find that some Germans were prepared to fight to the last man:

'B Company advanced 100 yards from objective. Then stopped by numerous pillboxes to front. Company C mortars and Company D mortars brought on targets but fail to neutralise pillboxes. Tanks were brought into position but failed to neutralise position. Assault teams sent forward; one from B Company, one from C Company. One AT platoon brought forward. Heavy fire from 57s laid on pillboxes. 2nd Platoon of D Company and LMGs of Company B brought on targets.'

It seemed as though nothing could penetrate the bunkers' thick walls and for several hours the GIs waited until a lucky shot exploded inside one pillbox. Seventeen dazed soldiers emerged waving a white flag and with their help the rest of position capitulated.

314th Regiment came under fire as it approached the railway station but once again tanks and anti-tank guns silenced the number of pillboxes. The Germans had already demolished part of the Gare Maritime's terminal by shunting a train packed with explosives into the building. Even so, Colonel Robinson had been warned to avoid the building following prisoner reports that it had been booby-trapped with delayed action mines.

By mid afternoon General Wyche was pleased to hear that his men had cleared the centre of Cherbourg and taken over 2,000 prisoners. Their work complete, the two Regiments retraced their steps, carrying out a second thorough search and posted guards at key road junctions en route. Meanwhile, Wyche passed on his congratulations: 'Division should feel cocky. 4th and 9th are both veteran Divisions and say it was a hard job to keep up with the 79th.'

314th Regiment's 2nd Battalion had remained on the roof of Fort du Roule all night and while the rest of 79th Division began to clear the city below, Colonel Huff's men renewed their attempts to take the lower levels. After failing to breach the doors, engineers began dropping explosive charges down ventilation shafts to encourage the men below to surrender. Attempts to reach the gun embrasures on the rock face had failed and after Lieutenant Kirby had withdrawn his men from the cliff, engineers lowered satchel charges from the roof of the fort. They used trigger devices to detonate the explosives, but still the 88s continued to fire on the city. Finally, eighteen tank-

Major-General Collins surveys the ruins of Cherbourg. NARA-111-SC-190981

The Stars and Stripes fly proudly in Cherbourg. NARA-111-SC-19034

destroyers lined up in the streets below and blasted the gun positions until they fell silent.

The garrison of the fort still refused to surrender. A frontal assault inside the fort would have resulted in heavy casualties and General Wyche felt it was time to try for a second time to reach the embrasures. Sergeant Hurst's team of volunteers climbed down the precipitous path, avoiding sniper fire as they crawled onto the cliff, and eventually found themselves over one of the embrasures. Pole charges failed to break open the steel shutters barring the way but with the help of a bazooka Hurst's men blasted the embrasure open. As the GIs peered warily into tunnel they could see white flags in the darkness; Fort du Roule had fallen and as night fell across Cherbourg, Colonel Robinson was able to report that the subterranean tunnels on the cliffs overlooking the city had been cleared. A naval officer and 178 men eventually emerged from the dark depths after keeping Colonel Huff's men at bay for forty-eight hours.

While the rest of 79th Division battled for Cherbourg, 315th

Major-General Eddy, with the assistance of a German speaking GI, cross-examines a senior German officer. NARA-111-SC-191083

Regiment finally cleared the pocket of resistance southwest of the city near Martinvast and Hardinvast. Patrols had located a large group of Germans and rather than engaging the enemy, Colonel Bernard B McMahon (the Regiment's commander since 24 June) had brought up a truck equipped with a loud speakers to pass on the news that General von Schlieben had surrendered. A German colonel made it clear in the negotiations that followed that he was anxious to maintain his honour; the Americans would have to exhibit an 'overwhelming display of strength' before he would surrender. Two white phosphorous grenades proved to be sufficient. The colonel surrendered with 1,200 men, the majority of them wounded in a nearby field hospital; hundreds of other soldiers were rounded up during the course of the day.

The Arsenal

Generalmajor Sattler had failed to response to ultimatums broadcast throughout the night and by the morning of 27 June, 47th Regiment was in position ready for the assault. Before launching his attack, Colonel Smythe made a final attempt to entice the Germans to surrender and a platoon from Company A approached the main gate, under the watchful eye of a Sherman tank. Small arms fire greeted the party and as they tried to withdraw, two 20mm AA guns came to life. The tank quickly destroyed them and as the platoon crawled back, General Eddy resigned himself to ordering the attack.

Men and tanks took up their positions waiting for zero hour but as the minutes ticked by, events began to quickly unfold. 47th Regiment's signal record details the final tense moments inside the Arsenal:

08:39 Blue artillery observers say somebody is getting ready to shoot on the Arsenal – wants it stopped – as white flag is up and a patrol is going in.

08:40 Something screwy is up in the Arsenal. Blue 6 can see soldiers evidently unarmed walking around on the ramparts. The doors are open.

08:50 Blue patrol is up to the gates of the moat, has had no fire whatsoever – bridge is blown out.

08:55 Patrols going in now – all fire missions have been cancelled. 1st and 3rd Battalions both report white flags flying over the Arsenal. Both bridges are blown and gates are open. Will have to get engineers up quickly in order to get in.

 09:10 General Eddy wants no troops to go into Arsenal until the Naval Engineers have been in for mines and demolitions inspection. Colonel Vanderhoef has four prisoners who can go in fort and accept surrender.

 09:25 Captain Jackson, Divisional G-2 and four prisoners are in the Arsenal right now. All battalions have been informed to hold patrols. Colonel Smythe is right outside the gates. General Eddy orders that if any American patrols have entered, withdraw them and hold them outside the gates.

 09:47 Prisoners are coming out of the Arsenal now – has seen about 50 so far and they are continuing to come in.

 09:56 Colonel Smythe in Arsenal – talking to Commandant – stubborn –

The capture of *Generalmajor* Sattler brought resistance in Cherbourg city to an end.
NARA-111-SC-190833-S/NARA-111-SC-190834-S

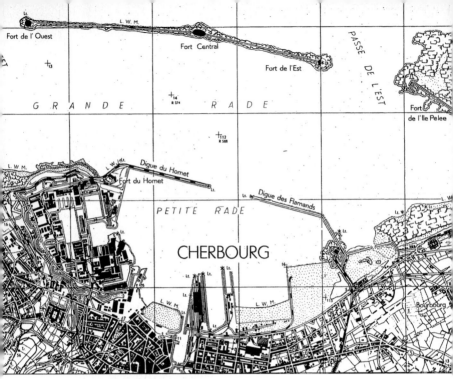

The final obstacle, Cherbourg's outer seawall.

has isolated groups of resistance throughout and he won't surrender until force is shown – tanks and tank destroyers are going down to every entrance.

10:10 Colonel Smythe is personally escorting the Naval Commander out of the Arsenal.

Four hundred men followed their leader into captivity, bringing to an end organised resistance on the mainland. During the past two days resistance had crumbled as ten 1,000 prisoners had ignored Hitler's order to hold Cherbourg to the last man.

Clearing the Breakwater

Once the mainland had been cleared, General Collins had to turn his attention to the forts protecting the outer harbour. Several sources had confirmed that the Germans had sown the harbour with mines:

'West of Fort Chavanac, generally in a semi circle to the south, there are a string of mines electrically operated by an unknown civilian. He has instructions to set off these mines after the harbour is full of Allied shipping. All entrances to the

160

harbour are heavily mined. A civilian diver reports that the harbours and outer breakwaters are extremely dangerous – mines, electronically operated and controlled – cannot be detected. Control points at Fort de l'Ouest and Fort Pelée. Heavy artillery positions on breakwaters.'

Although VII Corps was only hours away from freeing the port, it looked as though it would take weeks to clear the harbour for Allied shipping.

German soldiers occupied three Napoleonic forts, Fort l'Ouest, Fort Central and Fort l'Est on the two-mile long breakwater protecting Cherbourg's outer harbour. Fort Chavagnac, the fortress protecting the western approaches had capitulated at the same time as the Arsenal. However, the fort on the eastern side of the harbour, Fort Ile de Pelée was still occupied by enemy troops.

Two metre thick walls made the structures virtually impervious from attack, and each of the five storeys (two above water and three below) were stacked with supplies of ammunition, food and water. The forts could hold out for weeks and General Collins would have to employ a careful balance of diplomacy and strength to encourage the Germans to surrender.

The French underground believed that Fort Ile de Pelée was the most susceptible to surrender due to its isolated position. On the afternoon of 27 June, Major Johnson of the 1/12th Regiment was given the task of taking the fort and while tank-destroyers tried to shell the garrison into submission Johnson's men collected sailboats capable of crossing the mine-infested harbour.

As the barrage came to an end, Major Johnson and Colonel Jackson (the Battalion's previous commander who had been badly burned a week earlier and was still swathed in bandages), made one final attempt to encourage the garrison to surrender. The two officers made their way along the narrow causeway carrying a fluorescent white panel and hailed the garrison through a loudspeaker. Several German officers came forward to talk and although the commanding officer was prepared to surrender the garrison, he refused to do so in daylight. The officer agreed to cross later that night at low tide when it was safer to navigate the minefield. It also meant that the garrison could be evacuated without being seen by the rest of the forts. Later that night his men were able to evacuate forty-five

Fort III de Pelée. NARA-111-SC-191500

German soldiers from Fort Ile de Pelée in rubber dinghies.

In the meantime Major Johnson watched for signs of life along the seawall from the roof of Fort du Flamands. Eventually a group of figures appeared on Fort l'Est and Johnson's signal operator flashed repeatedly signally an ultimatum to surrender in Morse code. The Germans studied the signals and although three explosions were heard deep in the bowels of the fort there was no reply, (Johnson would later discover that no one could decipher the signals). There was still no sign of any white flags and as Johnson tried to re-establish contact with the forts, a salvo of shells from a company of 105mm howitzers brought the negotiations to an abrupt halt.

General Collins summoned Major-General Barton and Major Johnson to Fort de Querqueville and as the three watched, men of the 12th Regiment set sail across the harbour in rubber dinghies. Machine-gun fire sent them heading back for safety, leaving the three commanders no option, the forts would have to be shelled into submission. Throughout the night tank-destroyers, artillery and anti-tank guns lined up along the quayside to join in the bombardment. Fort Central burst into

162

flames as one shell hit an ammunition store, but even the shells of the 155mm Long Tom howitzers failed to penetrate the walls of the three forts.

Warships closed in ready to shell the seawall and while Major Johnson's men prepared to cross the harbour for a second time, General Collins arranged an attack by fighter-bombers timed to begin at 11:00am. As zero hour approached, soldiers began to emerge from Fort l'Ouest waving a white flag. It was too late to cancel the air strikes and as soon as planes appeared the Germans hurried inside. It looked as though an opportunity had been missed but as the dust settled, white flags appeared on the roof of Fort l'Est. An hour later Fort l'Ouest followed, bringing the battle for the seawall to an end.

Company A's commander, Captain Glenn W Thorne, sailed across the harbour to Fort l'Ouest and as his men looked on, the garrison performed one final ceremony. Two ranks of German soldiers lined up and saluted their injured officer as he emerged from the fort. He later explained how a single shell splinter had pierced a gun aperture and damaged the fort's generator rendering the control device for the minefield useless; the same splinter had also caused his own injuries.

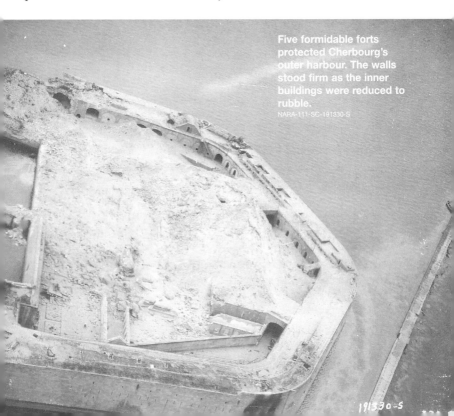

Five formidable forts protected Cherbourg's outer harbour. The walls stood firm as the inner buildings were reduced to rubble.
NARA-111-SC-191330-S

General Collins explains to General Bradley how his men captured Cherbourg.

NARA-111-SC-191143

Cherbourg's Liberation is complete

Although pockets of resistance still had to be cleared on the Cotentin Peninsula, General Collins decided to hold a liberation ceremony for the people of Cherbourg. At 16:00 a crowd of civilians gathered in the Place de la Republique and watched as their mayor accepted the freedom of the city:

'It was a typically American scene, perhaps typical of Frenchmen as well as Americans. Several hundred American soldiers and officers were standing on the street and balconies around the square. These free soldiers far outnumbered the men in ranks and

The presentation of flags: here we see the Stars and Stripes. Also presented were the Royal Navy's Ensign and the French Tricolour. NARA-111-SC-190745

A French Gendarme salutes the passing parade.
NARA-111-SC-191033

outnumbered the too few civilians, for Cherbourg was almost emptied of its population.'

A ceremonial band led the procession as the three divisional commanders marched into the square at the head of a platoon from each of their commands; VII Corps commander, General 'Lightning' Joe Collins came next:

'[He] *arrived in an M8* [armoured car], *dismounted without ceremony, and greeted the mayor on the steps of the haggard Hotel de Ville. A large group of generals, staff officers and a few French officials were clustered around. Overhead floated the British, French and American flags... General Collins presented to the mayor a French flag made from American parachutes (the colour of blue was off, being a sea green). The mayor gave a brief speech, and then General Collins read a five-minute speech in excellent French, concluding with 'Vivé la France'. Not satisfied with the vigour with which he had pronounced these words he repeated in a shout 'Vivé la France.' The small crowd gave its wholehearted applause... The band*

165

struck up a lively march. A young Frenchman across the square sprang into a lively Apache dance. The crowd closed around him, applauding. Those farther away ran towards this centre of interest. Then from all over the square the French men and women were running faster and more excitedly. American soldiers were shocked. The band and the dance stopped, the crowds dissolved. These people craved excitement and they had not had it.'

For many, the fact that they had been liberated was only just beginning to sink in. For four long years they had lived under the oppression of the German occupation. It would take a long time to restore their wrecked town to its former glory but they were free. The liberation of Europe was underway.

After four years of occupation Cherbourg is finally free. NARA-111-SC-191033

CHAPTER ELEVEN

The Final Pockets of Resistance

Maupertus Airport and Cap Lévy

Hill 158 had been held by 22nd Regiment since 21 June, protecting 4th Division's right flank from the German forces positioned around Maupertus airfield. For four days the Regiment had fought to keep its supply line open using tanks to escort soft vehicles along the road to Le Thiel. Once 12th Regiment reached the coast east of Cherbourg, Major-General Barton was able to turn his attentions to clearing the northeast corner of the Cotentin Peninsula where over 2,000 of the enemy had gathered at Maupertus airfield and Cap Lévy. On the evening of 25 June Colonel Robert T Foster (22nd Regiment's new commander), ordered his battalions to turn east to prepare to capture the airfield. Although the Cherbourg garrison had capitulated, the men at Maupertus were prepared to fight on:

'Instructions previously issued by the German commander had designated the airport as a centre of a last ditch resistance, all German soldiers who might be separated from their units were directed to make their way to the airport. The prisoners finally taken in this area had a high percentage of young Nazis. This sector was the most highly fortified area in the peninsula.'

22nd Regiment attacked the airfield on the morning of 26 June, encountering heavy fire from the cordon of anti-aircraft batteries built to protect the airstrip. Progress was slow, 22nd Regiment had lost many of its anti-tank guns and mortars over the past week and replacements had been hard to come by. Foster's infantry had come to rely on 44th Field Artillery Battalion for close support and over the past week the GIs had learnt many lessons:

'... all the troops had learned the value of manoeuvring. A platoon would no longer butt their heads straight in against an enemy strong point. When they run into heavy opposition now they move around a flank and get on commanding ground where they can look down the throat of an enemy. All of the old men have become so conscious of the value of communication that whenever one of them sees a broken wire he will immediately

crawl up and repair it... all of the old men learned how to observe for enemy fire. Men who spotted a hostile gun would take an azimuth reading from high ground or some other definite terrain feature then would move back to another identifiable feature and take a compass reading, then would gallop back to the artillery observer and say to him "this is where it is".'

The German positions were cleared one by one and by nightfall 3rd Battalion had captured Maupertus village, overrunning the AA batteries on the north side of the airfield. 2nd Battalion captured a heavily guarded battery of 40mm anti-aircraft guns on the western perimeter, while 1st Battalion cleared Gonneville and closed in on the southern edge of the airstrip. The remaining Germans around Maupertus capitulated the following morning.

Colonel Foster now had to turn his attentions to Cap Lévy where over 1,000 German troops had gathered to man the coastal batteries, including one of the largest on the peninsula, Fort Hamburg. The only consolation was that the batteries main armament were pointing out to sea. Even so, Foster's men faced

A ring of bunkers and trenches protected Fort Hamburg.
NARA-111-SC-191501

a network of pillboxes, entrenchments and flak guns:

> 'This was the most highly fortified area encountered in the whole peninsula. The position around the 200 foot radar tower contained twenty bunkers, each of which had three or four rooms. There was a large underground mess hall, which accommodated 500 men; elaborate periscopes covered all that position of the peninsula to the coast and permitted the numbers to be read on ships at sea. They were elaborate, extremely efficient fire control devices.'

As 3rd Battalion turned north and advanced towards the position it came under fire from anti-aircraft guns around the Napoleonic Fort at Cap Lévy. Captain Blassard, Company L's commanding officer, crawled forward onto a promontory overlooking the fort and radioed the coordinates to 44th Field Artillery Battalion. After a few salvoes, white flags appeared and Blassard went forward to meet the commandant of the fort, Major Kauppers. Later that evening Colonel Teague accepted the formal surrender of Cap Lévy and when Kauppers was asked why he had capitulated so quickly, he replied, 'Panzers to the right of me, panzers to the left of me, panzers in front of me, troops everywhere.'

Nearly 300 German soldiers were taken prisoner and as it was too late to evacuate them, Colonel Teague ordered them to assemble in the fort's mess hall:

> 'The prisoners requested that they be allowed to return to their bunkers for their blankets. Colonel Teague refused, but allowed them to go to the mess hall and remain there for the night, unguarded. Major Kauppers was a 'decent Joe' and he entertained the American officers with beer and cheese. He [Colonel Teague] wanted to be sure that the rest of the fortifications stayed surrendered and didn't start raising hell again the next day.'

Fort Hamburg refused to capitulate until the following morning; 990 men eventually surrendered to Colonel Teague, bringing resistance on the northeast tip of the peninsula to an end.

Cap de la Hague

During the final stages of the attack on Cherbourg, 60th Regiment had been keeping a watchful eye on the enemy troops on Cap de la Hague. Intelligence suggested that over 3,000 troops, organised into two *Kampfgruppen* led by *Oberstleutnant* Mueller and *Oberstleutnant* Keil, had gathered there. Despite continued shelling and air attacks they appeared to be preparing to make a stand. 919th and 922nd Regiments formed the backbone of the German forces, but, many of the troops trapped in the peninsula were artillery and service personnel with dubious fighting qualities. Reports from prisoners and civilians indicated that morale was low and General Eddy intended to use pamphlets and public address systems to entice as many as possible to surrender.

Colonel Rohan's men had reconnoitred the positions covering Hainneville, Ste Croix-Hague and Vauville, but once American troops had started to enter the city the Germans had fallen back to a shorter line between Querqueville and Branville. 60th Regiment followed, taking over 300 prisoners, three 88s and a battery of 105mm guns.

Following the fall of the Arsenal on the morning of 27 June, 47th Regiment moved up alongside 60th Regiment and as Colonel Smythe's men moved into Hainneville, P47 fighter-bombers targeted suspected enemy strongholds around Querqueville, Gruchy, Nacqueville and Jobourg. The Germans evacuated Querqueville soon afterwards and as Smythe's 2nd Battalion moved in to investigate, they came across 300 soldiers wishing to surrender. The fighter-bombers returned the following day and their attacks against the coastal batteries and Beaumont-Hague, paved the way for 9th Division's advance.

60th Regiment found that its first objective, Branville-Hague, had been abandoned but as Colonel Rohan's men advanced on Beaumont-Hauge they found that the Germans were preparing to make a stand. An anti-tank ditch barred the way and as 1st Battalion approached the road junction south of the village carefully concealed positions opened fire:

> 'B and C advanced about 300yds, C about 300 yards short of B. C Company said they can hold where they are, he is down in a gully. Tough from the left flank, tank fire or something and machine gun fire, things were fine for 300yds then ran into trouble. Fired all artillery we can fire. A Company on the right to try and get up to B.

As 1st Battalion engaged the strongpoint, 3rd Battalion attacked the German line north of the highway. The infantry worked their way forward pinpointing enemy positions for their tanks and artillery. The Germans retaliated. Launching a counterattack supported by tanks, and with the help of artillery fire Colonel Rohan's men held their positions. As darkness fell it was obvious that the two battalions had failed to break the German positions and neither of them were able to break off contact.

47th Regiment found that the Germans had withdrawn along the north coast, evacuating Urville-Nacqueville to take up positions east of Gréville-Hague. 3rd Battalion followed finding it a struggle to make headway along the rugged coastline: 'Road network is poor – there is congestion of vehicles on the road – they are narrow and there is danger of mines.'

The Germans had occupied a ridge overlooking the coast road but as 3rd Battalion advanced up the hill, the majority fled. After clearing the outlying trenches Companies K and L came under heavy fire from three anti-tank guns and a number of machine guns. A heavy artillery concentration shattered the Germans' morale and once the last round of smoke had been fired 3rd Battalion charged the position, taking sixty prisoners.

Colonel Smythe had heard conflicting reports about the positions guarding Gréville-Hague. Civilians reported that they were strongly held, but prisoners believed that the garrison was

9th Division's final attack on Beaumont Hague and Gréville Hague.

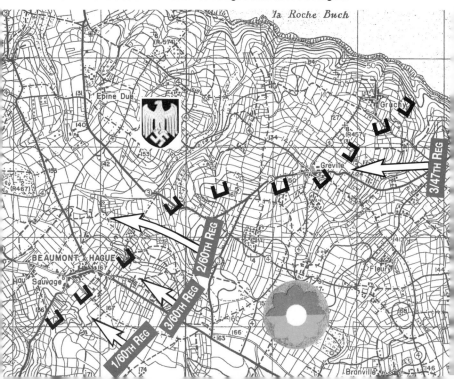

low on ammunition. An appeal to surrender produced twenty prisoners but patrols could still see signs of movement in the village. Smythe postponed the attack until the morning and during the course of the night a patrol captured thirty prisoners. They were able to confirm that their comrades had slipped away leaving Gréville-Hague unoccupied.

At first light on 29 June, Colonel Rohan's 2nd Battalion was in position ready to turn the flank of the German line covering Beaumont-Hauge. Company E had to wait for an hour while engineers filled in an anti-tank ditch and by the time the advance began, the artillery smoke screen had faded away. Captain Sprindus and Lieutenant Cookson (the only two surviving company officers) led their men across a minefield under heavy fire. 1st and 2nd Platoon charged straight at the German strongpoint allowing 3rd Platoon to slip unseen into Beaumont-Hague via a streambed. The sight of American troops in the village, behind their lines, led the Germans to believe that their line had been broken. Company F took advantage of the confusion caused and entered the village accompanied by Sherman tanks.

Meanwhile, 47th Regiment overran, or destroyed by artillery, machine gun posts and mortar positions around Gréville-

Ambulances move in while infantry clear the ruined streets of a burning village. NARA-111-SC-190403

The Germans pressed every shape and size of gun into action.
NARA-111-SC-191314

Hague and Hameau Gruchy. Once the two villages had been cleared, resistance began to crumble allowing Colonel Smythe to push west towards Cap de la Hague. The fall of Beaumont-Hague signalled the collapse of German morale opposite 60th Regiment's front and by nightfall Jobourg, three miles to the west, had fallen.

General Eddy wanted to finish clearing the peninsula as

German soldiers comtemplate their future in a prisoner of war camp.
NARA-111-SC-190978

quickly as possible but when he heard that the German officers were refusing to let their men lay down their arms, he decided to take the peninsula by force. Later that evening a company of tank-destroyers and a reconnaissance platoon joined the 3/39th Regiment, motorised for the occasion. Under cover of darkness the column set off towards Auderville on the tip of the peninsula. Hundreds of soldiers surrendered along the way and by dawn Lieutenant-Colonel Stumpf was able to report that he had cleared the village and captured the German commander *Oberst* Keil. 'Everything here gave up, Germans are just sitting around awaiting to be taken.'

The rest of 9th Division had spent the night mopping up their respective areas, taking over 3,000 prisoners. It brought the total taken to 6,000; double the initial estimate. The amount of ordnance discovered on the peninsula was also staggering: two railway guns, four 155mm howitzers, five 88s, two 47mm and ten 20mm flak guns were taken.

The Aftermath

At 15:00 on 1 July 1944, General Eddy reported that resistance had ended on Cap de la Hague Peninsula, bringing the Cherbourg campaign to a close. It was D+25, four days later

The capture of Cherbourg was a relief for General Eisenhower and Allied Supreme Headquarters. NARA-111-SC-19115

Life returns to normal, the first open market in Cherbourg
NARA-111-SC-191243

than planned but the delay was far less than Hitler had expected. He had ordered General von Schlieben to fight to the last man, yet 20,000 had surrendered, the majority in the final hours of the battle. VII Corps casualties in the thirteen-day campaign were over 8,800 men killed, wounded or missing; the German losses were far higher. The combination of infantry, armour, artillery and air attacks coupled with aggressive, and sometimes daring, tactics had overcome one of the strongest sections of the Atlantic Wall. Many of the lessons learnt on the Cotentin Peninsula, in particular the specialised tactics required to advance through the 'bocage' countryside, would be used time and time again in the Normandy campaign.

Hitler's recriminations came quickly. General von Schlieben, (now on his way across the English Channel into captivity), was denounced for his poor leadership of the troops under his command at Cherbourg. General Gerd von Rundstedt was ordered to court martial General Friedrich Dollmann, Seventh Army's commander, for his failure to drive the Americans back into the sea. However, on 29 June, as American troops were clearing the streets of Cherbourg, Dollmann died of a heart

175

attack; General von Rundstedt was removed from his post a few days later.

The capture of the port was a relief for the Allied Supreme Headquarters. Elsewhere on the Normandy front the advance inland was progressing far slower than expected. VIII Corps was experiencing its own difficulties in coming to terms with the Normandy 'bocage' around St Lô, while the British and Canadians were bogged down in front of Caen to the east. Now that VII Corps had cleared the Cotentin Peninsula, General Bradley could concentrate on breaking the German line to the south. 79th Division and 4th Division were already on their way, leaving the defence of Cherbourg to 101st Airborne Division, 9th Division would soon follow. Although the Cherbourg campaign was over, it was only the beginning of the liberation of Northwest Europe.

Throughout the weeks that followed engineers worked continuously to repair Cherbourg's port facilities, destroyed in the final hours of the battle, while navy divers cleared mines and obstacles from the harbour. By the end of the summer ships and amphibious craft of every shape and size were sailing into the port, bringing men, equipment and materials for the advance across northern France. At long last the Allies' reliance on the temporary harbour at Arromanches for supply had ended.

Weary troops of the 79th Division head south to their next battle
NARA 111-SC-191912

CHAPTER TWELVE

Touring Cherbourg

Three car tours covering the final battle for *Festung* Cherbourg follow and each one approximately covers one division's attack on the fortress. Although there are maps in the book, it would be wise to purchase the relevant road maps of the area. The most detailed are the Série Bleu Maps; Reference Number 1210E (Cherbourg) and Cap de Hague Reference Number 1110E (or 1210 OT). IGN 1:1000,000 scale No.6, Caen/Cherbourg is also useful.

Remember that the French drive on the right and on narrow lanes a driver's right of way is a matter of courtesy. The terrain surrounding Cherbourg is dominated by *bocage*, high earth embankments topped with thick hedgerows lining many of the roads and lanes, and this makes navigation a challenge at the best of times. Turning round if you miss a junction is rarely an option (and dangerous in many of the narrow lanes) and it is usually some distance before you can contemplate retracing your steps. If you do become lost, follow signposts to a village and stop to study the map. It will then be possible to head back to the last point on the route that you remember.

Ferry Terminal to the Harbour

When you leave the port take the first right at the roundabout, signposted for Cherbourg (Centre Ville) and after 400 metres the harbour basin appears as the road bends to the left. Turn right at the traffic lights, entering Cherbourg's one-way system, and cross the bridge between the inner and outer basins; the **Tourist Information Centre (Maison du Tourisme)** is on the far side of the bridge and it is the **starting point for all three tours**. A 1944 comparison can be seen on page 153.

There is ample on-street parking (payable by the hour at road side meters) in the centre of Cherbourg. However, market days can be very busy. Many of the streets in the old town, immediately to the west of the harbour, are pedestrian precincts and should be avoided until you have parked your vehicle.

Either follow signs or ask for directions to the harbour if you need to visit the Tourist Information Office. The majority of the staff do speak English and it is an excellent place to ask any unusual questions if you not confident with French. Many of the locals in the town speak a little English but

Fort du Roule overlooks Cherbourg's harbour.

once you leave the port you will need to speak French to be understood.

There are a variety of hotels of all standards in and around Cherbourg and a comprehensive list is available at the Tourist Office. It is also possible to search for hotels on the internet and some take online bookings. Cherbourg is a popular tourist area and it can get booked up in the summer season and school holidays. It is particularly busy around the anniversaries of D-Day at the beginning of June and the liberation at the end of the month. Useful road signs printed in red give directions to many of the hotels in the town centre.

Car Tour 1 – 4th Division

Follow the one-way system from the Tourist Information office, heading inland alongside the inner harbour. At the end of the harbour basin follow **signs for Caen, Rennes and Tourlaville**, turning left at the traffic lights. Turn right at a second set of traffic lights after 200m and follow the N13, signposted for Caen and Rennes, heading south out of Cherbourg. The road follows a narrow valley, with Fort du Roule on the cliff to the left, and climbs steeply as it heads out of the suburbs. Go straight on at the roundabout after 2 1/2 miles in Cherbourg's commercial area and continue straight on at a second roundabout after another 1/2 mile. Take the **slip road to the right** after two miles, signposted for **Delasse** and the D56.

79th Division ran into *Kampfgruppen* Koehn's outposts as it approached Delasse on 20 June, coming under fire from 88s, mortars and artillery ①. Turn **left at the crossroads** signposted for **Le**

Car Tour 1 - 4th Division's area.

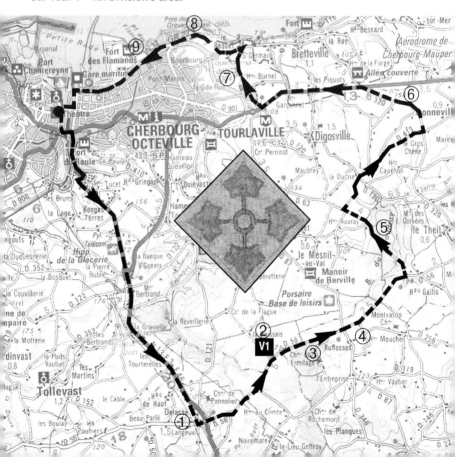

Delasse crossroads where 313th Regiment was ambushed by 88mm guns.

Theil and cross over the dual carriageway. Hedgerows and woods close in around the D56 as it heads east and it easy to see why the Normandy 'bocage' was ideal defensive terrain. 8th Regiment advanced from right to left as it headed towards the Trottebec valley, encountering German strongpoints in the patchwork of small enclosures. Colonel van Fleet repeatedly struggled to coordinate attacks with his supporting armour and German troops frequently infiltrated behind the Regiment's lines.

After 1 ¹/₂ miles, at the end of a long straight, there is a concrete track to the left marked by a small signpost for La Boissaie. In the fields to the left of the road are a number of bunkers and the remains of a V1 launch ramp ②.
8th Regiment encountered strong German position in Bois du Rondou (now called Foret de l'Ermitage) to the right of the road.

Continue east and at the end of the wood, there are a number of concrete shelters in the trees to the right of the road ③; further evidence of the extensive V1 rocket activity in this area. Crossroads 148 is a short distance further on. ④

Bunkers and shelters surround the V1 launch r captured by 8th Regiment.

While the rest of 8th Regiment was heavily engaged in Bois du Rondou to the right of the road, two companies of 2nd Battalion were pinned down as they advanced across the fields to the left. Lieutenant-Colonel MacNeely used unusual tactics to break the deadlock, deploying a 'tank platoon in line, an infantry platoon immediately behind each tank, the whole line charged, tanks firing guns and machine-guns, infantry spraying with all their machine-guns.' In spite of clearing the fields north of Bois du Rondou, German troops infiltrated behind MacNeeely's position using the houses at Crossroads 148 as a base. The following morning Captain Kulp was sent back to deal with the threat and found the enemy sheltering in a copse north of the crossroads. After pulverising the wood with mortars, howitzers and machine

Shelters lie hidden in Bois du Rondou.

Crossroads 148, the base for German counterattacks on 8th Regiment's rear.

guns; Kulp's men rounded up 250 prisoners.

Head straight on **towards Le Theil** and turn left onto the D63 after a mile, heading into **Bois du Coudray**. The road drops steeply down to the Saire stream on the far side of the wood where 12th Regiment found the Germans waiting on the slopes across the valley ⑤. The bridge had already been destroyed and marshy ground either side of the stream prevented Colonel Luckett deploying his tanks. It took two days to find suitable crossing point downstream.

Continue across the stream, turning right onto the D413 towards Gonneville after 1/2 mile. Keep straight on at the crossroads after 1/2 mile taking note of the high hedgerows surrounding the enclosures either side of the road. Having found a crossing over the Saire, Captain Linder led his men along this road to outflank the German positions blocking 12th Regiment's advance. Sherman tanks had to keep to the road, turning into the fields when Linder's men identified an enemy position.

After 1 1/4 mile **turn left onto the D320**, heading north. The high ground immediately in front is Hill 158 ⑥. 22nd Regiment

The Saire stream provided a natural defensive position on the north edge of Bois du Coudray.

made a rapid advance along this road on the evening of 21 June, seizing the hill and cut Maupertus airfield off from Cherbourg. Over the next four days German infantry repeatedly attacked supply trucks as they tried to reach the Regiment's positions. Major-General Barton eventually resorted to sending tanks stacked with ammunition and food to keep the Regiment supplied.

Turn **left onto the D901** after 1 mile; note that the road climbs to the summit of Hill 158 as it heads east towards Maupertus airfield. Heading west, with Cherbourg in the distance, the importance of 22nd Regiment's position on the high ground is clear. There is a water tower on the left after 1 1/2 mile; turn right onto the D120, signposted for Hameau Burnel and stop at a small parking area to the right

The road to Maupertus was the scene for many ambushes after 22nd Regiment had made its lightning drive to capture Hill 158.

after 400m. Cross the road and walk along Rue Fournel; after 200m climb the grassy mound to the left of the lane to see 4th Division's view of Cherbourg ⑦.

General Collins, Major-General Barton and Colonel Luckett watched from near here as 12th Regiment pushed along the coast into the city. Tourlaville is immediately in front, with Fort du Roule on the promontory straight ahead. Cherbourg's harbour is to the right with the breakwater forming a huge arc out in the sea. Return to your car and head **continue along the D120** towards the sea. The brambles and gorse bushes area to the left of the road conceals a number of bunkers and shelters that once formed a large underground hospital. The road drops steeply down a narrow ravine as it heads for Le Becquet and towards the bottom of the slope it is possible to see Fort Ile de Pelée out to sea.

At the bottom of the hill, turn left at the traffic lights in Le Becquet and head towards Cherbourg. Take the first right at the roundabout after 1/2 miles heading for the sea front and turn left signposted for Plage Colignon after 400m. The road makes a sharp right turn in front of the bypass and heads towards the beach. There is a large bunker at the T Junction on the sea front, park next to it to take a closer look at the harbour.

Fort Ile de Pelée ⑧ is the closest, covering the eastern approach to the harbour. Major Johnston walked out along the

Hill 158, on the St Pierre Église road, dominated the countryside.

A lone bunker overlooks the port.

The road into Le Becquet; the seawall protects Cherbourg's outer harbour.

A bunker looks out to sea; Fort Ile de Pelée is in the distance.

thin walkway towards the fort to negotiate with the garrison. The garrison delayed their surrender until it was dark, fearing reprisals from the rest of the forts. Having taken Fort Ile de Pelée it took thirty-six hours and bombardments from the land, sea and the air to convince the men on the sea wall to capitulate.

Continue west, towards the centre of Cherbourg. Fort des Flamands ⑨ can be seen to the right as you drive along the sea front. Take the first exit at the roundabout, heading for Cherbourg Centre. The road heads past the port entrance and back into the centre of the town.

Car Tour 2 – 79th Division

The first mile of tour two is the same as the previous tour. Follow the one-way system along the harbour and turn left at the traffic lights at the end, **turn right at the second set of lights** and head up the valley between Fort du Roule and Octeville. Go straight on at the first traffic lights, turning right, signposted for **Bricquebec**, at a second set of lights after 200m. The photograph alongside symbolises the capitulation of Cherbourg; the large sign is on the retaining wall to the left of the traffic lights.

La Glacerie is the next village and after 1/2 mile, just after two sharp bends, **turn left** onto the D119, heading up a steep slope. **La Loge** is at the top of the hill; park you car in the centre of the hamlet just before a stop sign on the right ①. Walk back along the road, taking note of the plaque across the road; it remembers sixteen local people who died while

• EN CE LIEU •
16 PERSONNES
ONT PAYÉ DE LEUR VIE
LA LIBERATION DU PAYS
*LE SOUVENIR FRANÇAIS
RECONNAISSANT*

Car Tour 2 - 79th Division's area.

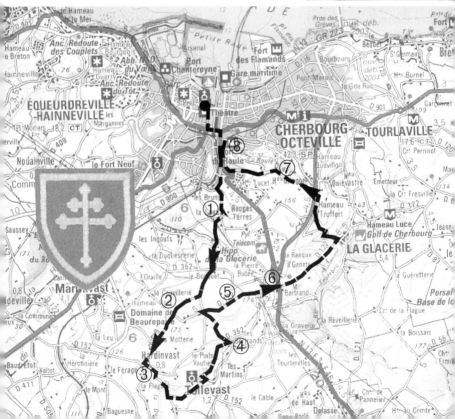

The road into Cherbourg...

fighting with the Resistance. Turn left into Chemin de la Chesnee after 50m and from the first gateway on the right it is possible to look over Cherbourg. The port is framed between the Octeville Heights and the Fort du Roule promontory. The difficulties faced by General Wyche and the men of 79th Division are obvious: both ridges had to be cleared before the 313th Regiment could ad-

...the view in June 1944 (top), prisoners are escorted into captivity. NARA-111-SC-190810-S

vance along the Divette valley. A single company of 314th Regiment penetrated the German lines to reach La Loge on 23 June; the GIs were the first ground troops to look on VII Corps final objective.

Return to your car and **continue along the D119**, heading for **Hardinvast**. Go straight on at the crossroads after two miles, taking note of the views to the right. Bois du Mont du Roc, a huge wooded hill dominates the horizon ②. As 9th Division cleared the hill, 315th Regiment set up roadblocks in this area to protect 79th Division's flank. Between them, the two divisions stopped over 3,000 German soldiers from retiring towards the port. They eventually capitulated on 26 June.

VII Corps final objective, the port of Cherbourg framed between the Octeville Heights and Fort du Roule as seen from La Loge.

Hardinvast is a mile further on; turn left at the church and park in front of the wall ③. The

Bois du Mont du Roc and Hill 171 overlooks Martinvast where thousands of German troops were cut off.

German troops holding Hardinvast had a perfect field of fire across 315th Regiment's advance.

church steps provide an ideal place to view the left flank of 79th Division's positions around St Martin le Gerard on 22 June. Allied planes bombed and strafed General Wyche's troops as they waited for zero hour on the far side of the valley and 315th Regiment ran into heavy opposition as it advanced. General Wyche decided to exploit the success on his right flank and left Colonel Wiggin's men to contain the Germans in Hardinvast. Over the days that followed 315th Regiment gradually extended its perimeter onto the high ground to the northeast, helping to encircle Hardinvast and Martinvast.

Return to your car and head **east along the D152,** following a right turn on the outskirts of the village; Tollevast is a mile away. In places it is possible to see the ridge to the left where German observers watched 79th Division's attack unfold and were able to call on mortars, anti-aircraft guns and artillery to stall the advance.

314th Regiment tried in vain to enter the Tollevast and attempts to outflank the village became pinned down in front of strong entrenchments. Eventually, Colonel Robinson had to withdraw his troops under cover of darkness and send them through the gap created by 313th Regiment to the east.

Carry straight on **past the Tollevast's Marie** and follow the D352 as it winds its way through the village. German engineers had turned the area into a fortress, building entrenchments, strongpoints and bunkers amongst the hedgerows. A short drive through this area, where at times it is narrow for a car to pass between the hedges, will leave a lasting impression on how formidable *Festung* Cherbourg was.

Continue on the D352, signposted for **La Glacerie**. There is a crossroads after ½ mile with a large bunker in the field on the right ④. Park in the area on the left just beyond the junction and take the opportunity to study, one of the few remaining examples of the dozens of pillboxes that covered this area in 1944. If you walk a short distance up the road to the right of the bunker it is possible to see the gun aperture and study the effects of the high explosives

One of the few surviving bunkers around Tollevast; the firing slit has been blown apart by explosives.

Looking south across 79th Division's assembly area.

used by the American troops.

Return to your car and turn round, turning right into the D511 signposted for **Martinvast**. Turn right at the top of the ridge onto the D112 heading for **La Glacerie** and park alongside the water tower on the left after ¼ mile ⑤. 313th Regiment finally broke the German fortifications at les Chèvres to the east on the evening of 22 June and reached this ridge under cover of darkness. Rather than batter his way through the defences at Hardinvast and Tollevast, General Wyche decided to exploit the breakthrough and ordered 314th Regiment to pull back from Tollevast. Overnight Colonel Robinson's men made their way onto the ridge with its commanding views both north and south, and took up positions ready for the German reaction. It never came. Apart from snipers and small groups harassing the supply columns, the Germans holding Tollevast melted away, looking to find a way back to Cherbourg. Wyche's daring plan had worked; the outer ring of entrenchments on his front had fallen.

Looking north from the water tower, it is possible to see the outskirts of Cherbourg and Octeville on the horizon. Although a hedge blocks the view over Tollevast, there is a gate a short walk along the road to the west. The view south, the one the German observers enjoyed, is also impressive. From here the importance of 79th Division's achievement on 22 June is obvious.

Return to your car and continue to **drive east along the ridge**; there is a second opportunity to view 79th Division's approach to Cherbourg from the small car park in front of an electricity substation on the right⑥. Looking across to the city, the main highway is to the right and Crossroads 177 is close to the water tower. 313th Regiment reached the crossroads on the night of 22 June, having pierced the German line at Les Chèvres. A commercial estate covers La Mare à Canards, the next line of German fortification north of the crossroads.

Continue straight on under the main highway and follow the D122 as it descends steeply into the Trottebec valley. While 313th Regiment moved forward under cover of darkness towards Crossroads 177, one battalion became disorientated in the woods to the right and lost contact with the rest of the Regiment. General Collins avoided sending troops into the Trottebec valley and while 79th Division exploited the success at Crossroads 177, 4th Division advanced across the high ground in the distance.

La Glacerie is a mile from the underpass; turn left at the bottom of the steep hill, signposted for La Glacerie Centre. Head **through the centre of La Glacerie** and turn left at the far end, making an immediate left beyond the underpass, (signposted for Valognes). Turn right at the T-junction after 200m and follow the side road up the hill. It is possible to park near the summit and look over the suburbs of Cherbourg and Tourlaville ⑦. The fields on the opposite side of the road were used as a base for German artillery. The gun crews ran for cover as 313th Regiment drew close; they were eventually rounded up in Hau Gringor quarry below. Once 314th Regiment had cleared the roof of Fort du Roule, 313th Regiment made its way down the slope heading into the suburbs; 4th Division approached from the right, taking Tourlaville by surprise under cover of darkness with infantry mounted on tanks.

Heading west in your car, the road descends rapidly into a narrow valley and Octeville, with its distinctive water tower, comes into view. 314th Regiment crossed this ravine to reach Fort du Roule on the summit of the ridge to the right of the road. Air strikes and an artillery bombardment failed to neutralise bunkers and entrenchments protecting the only approach to the fort and 314th

Regiment's first attempt to cross the valley failed. A second attack succeeded in gaining a foothold on the slope, in spite of enfilade fire from the Octeville heights.

Continue through La Glacerie to the bottom of the hill and turn right onto the main road into Cherbourg. Once 314th Regiment had started to ascend the ridge, 313th Regiment advanced astride this road heading for the centre of Cherbourg. Lieutenant Ogden was awarded the Congressional Medal of Honour for single-handedly destroying two machine guns and an anti-aircraft position on the steep slope to the right.

Head **straight on at the traffic lights** and take the first right after the pedestrian crossing, signposted for Fort du Roule and Museé de la Liberation. The second turning to the right after 100m leads up the hill to the fort. A narrow road with passing places winds its way up the cliff, making a number of severe turns. There are parking spaces at the summit ⑧.

Fort du Roule

The museum entrance fee is three euros (concessions 1.5 euros) and opening times are:

July to September	Tuesday to Saturday	11:00 to 18:00
	Sunday and Monday	14:00 to 18:00
October to May	Wednesday and Sunday	14:00 to 18:00
	Other days	10:00 to 12:00

As you enter the courtyard of the fort through the original Napoleonic gate note that Company E of 314th Regiment approached from the right, having cleared pillboxes covering the promontory. Corporal Kelly was awarded the Congressional Medal of Honour for clearing one pillbox single-handedly. The entrance to the museum is at the far and of the modern glass structure but before you enter the museum take time to view the incredible panorama from the balcony; the information board at the end indicates all the landmarks. On a clear day it is possible to see the whole of Cherbourg and its suburbs, from Octeville in the west round to Tourlaville in the east. Having taken the courtyard of the fort, Company E hoped that the Germans below would surrender. However, over 150 men continued to fight on, harassing the troops advancing into the city. Looking over the parapet, it is possible to see one of the pillboxes on the cliff face. Engineers tried lowering satchel charges to dislodge the Germans but it took a barrage from eighteen tank-destroyers, gathered on the streets below, to silence them. Only then could Sergeant Hurst and a party of volunteers climb along the cliff face to reach the gun embrasures below and enter the fort.

The museum contains a large selection of photographs, artefacts and film archive recalling life in Cherbourg during the Second World War. The German occupation, life under the Nazis, the French resistance, VII Corps' liberation of the city and the rebuilding of the port are dealt with in turn on the upper two floors of the fort. The only disadvantage is that the captions are in French.

After visiting the museum drive down to the bottom of the hill turning left towards the main road into the city and return to the Tourist Information Centre.

Cherbourg; the impressive panorama from Fort du Roule.

Car Tour 3 – 9th Division

Follow the one-way system from the Tourist Information Office, alongside the inner harbour, and go straight on at the traffic lights, signposted for **Octeville**. Head up the hill onto Octeville heights, which were covered in anti-aircraft positions in 1944, and go straight on at the traffic lights at the top, following the road out of the suburbs. To the left of the road is the Divette valley where several thousand German soldiers held out for several days. The village of Le Pont is one mile beyond Octeville; take the first exit at the roundabout, heading straight on towards Les Pieux. Bois du Mont du Roc is across the valley to the right of the road and as you head south west it is easy to see why 9th Division did not push men onto the lower slopes of the hill; the infantry trapped around Martinvaast to the left of the road had an excellent field of fire across the valley.

Slow down once you have passed the turning for Sideville to the right. The turning you want is also to the right and although it is signposted for Flottemanville-Hague, **the sign is facing the wrong way** (a sign for Hardinvaast is directly opposite). After crossing the Divette Steam the road climbs towards Les Vacheaux. Go straight on at the crossroads in the centre of the hamlet after 1/2 mile; signposted for Flottemanville-Hague. The road bends sharply to the right as it climbs the hill; park in the entrance to a track on the left after 100 metres ①. A short walk along the track gives you the opportunity to see the German perspective of 47th Regiment's advance across the Houelbecq stream. The stream winds its way through the wooded valley below and the Germans holding the high ground to the right and behind your position could see Colonel Smythe's as they advanced on 22 June. The steep sided valley prevented armour moving forward to support the infantry as they struggled to find a way through the minefields and barbed wire either side of the stream.

Car Tour 3 - 9th Division's area.

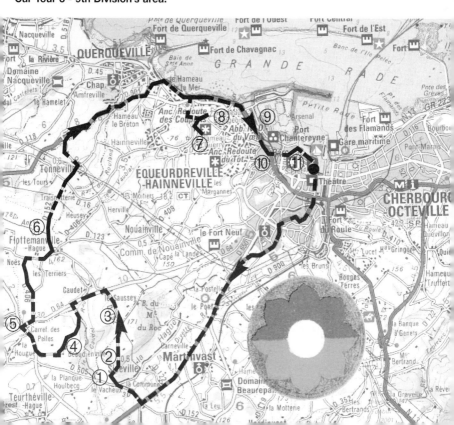

The anti-aircraft positions at Strongpoint 13 now serve as picnic areas.

Return to your car and **continue up the hill**, parking to the right after 200 metres opposite three concrete shelters built to resemble houses ②. If you look over the fence there are a number of bunkers to the right of the 'houses'. The complex served an anti-aircraft position on the top of the hill; the gun positions had a commanding view across 9th Division's advance.

Continue to drive up the hill and ½ mile further on is a pull in to the right where two tracks head off up the hill ③. The stopping point gives you the opportunity to take in another view across the Houelbecq valley and Baudienville beyond; Hill 171 and Bois du Mont du Roc are to the right of the road. From here it is possible to appreciate the difficult task facing General Eddy's men.

Continue straight on and as the road starts to descend it is possible to see Flottemanville-Hague, with its white church spire, on the horizon. Strongpoints around the village had a commanding view of 9th Division's advance. **Turn left at Le Saussey crossroads** and the road descends rapidly towards the Houelbecq steam. The strongpoint around the crossroads stalled 47th Regiment's advance until tanks could be directed forward, meanwhile, parties of Germans cut off by the advance continued to harass supply trucks along the road. The road crosses Houelbecq steam at the bottom of the hill. **Turn left into the narrow lane just beyond the bridge** and follow it into Baudienville. 47th Regiment advanced from the village on 22 June under heavy fire from the strongpoints on the high ground to the left. The breakthrough came when the artillery hit the ammunition dump of one strongpoint, allowing the infantry to move close enough to assault. The rest of the Regiment exploited the breakthrough and moved onto the high ground under cover of darkness.

As you follow the narrow road **through Baudienville** ④ the difficulties faced by Colonel Smythe and his supporting armour are clear. 400m beyond the village **turn right onto the D22**.

Turn right at the next crossroads, Crossroads 114 ⑤, signposted for Octeville. 47th Regiment's 2nd Battalion ran into heavy fire from pillboxes at the crossroads on 22 June, they were eventually overcome when tank destroyers moved up, giving covering fire as the GIs charged the bunkers.

Take the **first left** after 400m and follow the road to the T-junction at the top of the hill; turn right into Flottemanville-Hague. **Turn left before the church**, signposted for **Tonneville**, and after 400m, turn left into the entrance for **'Ludiver'** ⑥, and park in the car park. The complex has a tourist information centre, a number of observatories and rotunda. It is built on the site of Strongpoint 13, an anti-aircraft position and the concrete emplacements now serve as picnic areas! The importance of the position is clear. The views along the coast are impressive and once the position had fallen, 9th Division was able to push towards Cherbourg. *Kampfgruppen* Keil withdrew from the strongpoint, and its rearguard surrendered as 60th Regiment attacked, closely supported by tank destroyers.

Return to your car and at the entrance to the site turn left down the hill. Head straight on at the crossroads after ½ mile into **Tonneville**. Turn left at the T Junction in the centre of the village and as you leave the houses behind, turn right onto the D901 signposted for Cherbourg. The dual carriageway descends quickly towards the sea. Go straight on at the traffic lights after 2 miles, signposted for **Hameau de la Mer**. Turn right for **Hainneville** at the roundabout on the sea front

after ½ mile. Turn **left at the traffic lights** after 300m and **right at a second set of lights** after 400m, signposted for **Fort des Couplets**. Turn left after 400m and the fort is a short distance away, behind a line of pine trees, beyond the parking area ⑦.

A preserved anti-aircraft position.

Fort des Couplets was one of the Napoleonic forts on the hills west of Cherbourg that had been upgraded by German engineers. 47th Regiment's 2nd Battalion attacked it after fighter-bombers, artillery and tank-destroyers had shelled the position; eighty-nine men surrendered after a brief battle. Pillboxes line the high earth embankments beyond the original moat.

Return to the road and turn right down the hill, retracing your route, however, head straight on at the crossroads and park alongside the open area, 150m on the left. There are three gun emplacements and an anti-aircraft position in the park.

Equeurdreville Battery illustrated how effective coastal batteries could be against naval targets⑧ on June 25, engaging the Allied task force as it sailed close to the shore. Salvoes from the battery damaged one ship and straddled several others before the flotilla's destroyers could lay a protective smoke screen. It took over 200 shells to silence the battery.

Return to your car, turn around and **at the crossroads turn right** and **again turn right** at the traffic lights after 1/4 mile, heading down to the roundabout towards the sea. Take the second exit, sign posted Cherbourg, and follow the dual carriageway along the sea front. The wall of the Arsenal⑨, the huge Napoleonic fortress built to protect Cherbourg's military port, is on the left after ½ mile. Anti-aircraft positions stand in front of the wall at the corner of the fort and it is possible to park close by if you wish to take a closer look.

47th Regiment reached the walls of the fortress on the afternoon of 26 June but 20mm AA guns on the walls prevented Colonel Smythe's men crossing the wide avenue. Tanks cruised up and down Rue Gambetta while attempts to contact *Generalmajor* Sattler were made. When all opportunities appeared to have been exhausted the order to attack was given but as Colonel Smythe's men prepared for the assault, white flags appeared and the doors to the fortress opened. Cherbourg's final mainland stronghold had surrendered.

There are a number of car parks in front of the Arsenal's walls if you wish to study the fortress and have a closer look at the German pillboxes. The dual carriageway continues towards the town centre passing a large white building, the Maritime Hospital, to the right ⑩. Over 2,500 wounded men, 150 of them captured US soldiers, were discovered inside the building. Place de la Republique is on the right in front of Cherbourg's main church after ½ mile ⑪.

Cherbourg's liberation ceremony took place in the square on the afternoon of 27 June and a small crowd gathered to watch as General Collins proclaimed the port free. The Hotel de Ville is on the right and a small plaque by the door remembers the first US soldier to reach the building on the night of 26 June. Twenty-year old Sergeant William F Finley was killed in action on 1 April 1945, four weeks before the war ended.

The main road past the church turns alongside the harbour and back to the Tourist Information Centre, completing your tour of *Festung* Cherbourg.

INDEX

Places

Acqueville 41, 69, 70, 72,
Anneville 37
Arromanches 67, 176
Auderville 174
Babeuf stream 27
Barneville-sur-Mer 19-21
Baudienville 56, 76, 188
Bayeux 9
Beaumont-Hague 170, 172-173
Biniville 19
Bois de la Brique 29, 31, 42
Bois du Coudray 46, 51, 62, 87, 88, 99, 180
Bois de Néretz 40
Bois du Mont du Roc 40, 50, 55, 76, 89, 93, 104, 105, 183, 187, 188
Bois du Rondou 48, 60, 61, 83, 86, 104, 179
Branville-Hague 170
Bricquebec 21, 26, 182
Brix 44
Cap de la Hague 39, 41, 53, 55, 104, 106, 121, 122, 147, 169-173
Cap Lévy 167-169
Carentan 9, 11, 14, 18
Carteret 25
Cherbourg
Arsenal 126, 143, 145, 147, 152, 158-160, 189
Boulevard Maritime 138
Canal de Retenue 153
Les Mielles area 138
Maritime Hospital 126, 143, 189
Place de la Republique 164, 189
Quai du Normandie 138
Rue Carnot 138
Rue de la Bretonnière 138
Rue Etienne Dolet 138
Rue Gambetta 143, 145, 189
Rue du General Leclerc 138
St Sauveur area 144, 147
Val de Saire area 153
Cotentin Peninsula 11, 32, 45, 49, 62, 68, 164, 167, 175,
Couville 27
Croix Jacobs 32, 44

Delasse 43, 178
Digosville 116, 117
Divette River 50, 53, 55, 76, 104, 125, 132, 147, 183, 186
Douve River 11, 13, 14, 18, 19, 22, 27, 29, 44
Flottemanville-Hague 41, 50, 54, 56, 69, 76, 89, 91, 106, 187, 188
Gloire River 31, 33, 42, 44
Gonneville 168, 180
Grande Huanville 19
Gréville-Hague 171, 172
Gruchy (Hameau Gruchy) 170, 172
Haumeau du Long 45
Hardinvast 42, 44, 46, 76, 80, 158, 183, 185
Hau du Long 43
Hau Gringor 111, 185
Helleville 27
Houelbecq stream 40, 41, 50, 73, 74, 76, 187, 188
Huberville 37
Jobourg 170, 173
La Bourdonnerie 61
La Brique 29-31, 42, 43
La Fière 14, 18
La Glacerie 110, 182, 185, 186
La Haye du Puits 19
La Loge 97, 182, 183
La Mare à Canards 94, 95, 97, 104, 108, 185
La Victoire 37
Le Becquet 136, 181
Le Ferrange 55
Le Ham 14
Le Saussy 74, 104
Le Thiel 48, 62, 64, 167
Le Vretot 26
Les Chèvres 76, 79-81, 185
Les Pieux 27
Lossiere 33
Maupertus 51, 62, 63, 104, 117, 167-169, 180
Merderet River 11, 14, 15
Le Mesnil-au-Val 100
Montebourg 14, 23, 24, 33, 38, 51
Nacqueville 170, 171
Nehou 19

Néretz stream 56
Omaha Beach 6, 9, 65-67
Orglandes 19
Pinabel 63
Querqueville 170
Quineville 14, 38
Rauville la Bigot 25, 27
Rocheville 27
St Christophe du Foc 27
Ste Colombe 19
Ste Croix-Hague 41, 44, 53-55, 70, 121, 170
St Germain le Gaillard 25, 27
St Jacques de Nèhou 21, 25
St Joseph 42
St Lô 176
St Pierre d'ArthÉglise 19
St Pierre Église 62, 63
St Sauveur-le-Vicomte 19
Ste Mere Église 6, 11
Saire stream 87, 88, 99, 100, 180
Samson 43
Saussemesnil 46, 48
Tamerville 46
Tollevast 44, 46, 76, 80, 81, 184, 185
Tonneville 107, 122, 188
Tourlaville 66, 101, 104, 111, 116-118, 134, 136, 178, 181, 185, 186
Trottebec stream 76, 94, 110, 111, 115, 134, 179, 185
Urville 31
Utah Beach 9, 11-13
Valognes 29, 31, 33, 42, 47
Valtot 55
Vauville 170
Strongpoints
Crossroads 114–41, 73, 74, 188
Crossroads 129–70, 72
Crossroads 133–71
Crossroads 148–60, 62, 82, 83, 179
Crossroads 177–81, 94, 185
Fort Central 161, 162
Fort de Chavagnac 142, 160, 162
Fort de Couplets 124, 189
Fort de l'Est 161, 162
Fort des Flamands 137, 138, 142, 162, 182
Fort Hainert 147

Fort Hamburg 168, 169
Fort Hameau du Tot 124
Fort Ill de Pelée 136, 161, 162, 181
Fort Neuf 105, 107, 126
Fort de l'Ouest 161, 163
Fort de Querqueville 162
Fort du Roule 66, 110-11, 119, 133, 136, 152, 153, 155-157, 178, 181, 185-186
Hill 110–35, 37
Hill 119–35, 37
Hill 128–190
Hill 138–90
Hill 140–101, 102
Hill 150–69-71, 90-91
Hill 151–104-106, 108
Hill 158–63-64, 134, 167, 180
Hill 160–71, 72, 91
Hill 170–39, 53
Hill 171–40, 50, 53, 76, 93-94, 104, 188
Hill 178–48
Hill 180–72, 91-92, 94, 106
Point 33–109
Point 34–109
Point 44–129
Point 45 (see Fort du Roule)
Point 46–110, 111, 130, 132
Redoubte des Fourches 108, 122, 124
Strongpoint 13–91-93, 188
Strongpoint 19–106-108
Strongpoint 190–111-115
Allied Personnel
Arnaud, Major 95
Barton, Major-General Raymond O 12, 13, 14, 23, 33, 37, 46, 47, 48, 59, 62, 63, 115, 134, 136, 137, 162, 167, 180,
Bibber, Lieutenant-Colonel Edwin M van 79
Blassard, Captain 169
Bradley, General Omar 9, 66, 121, 152, 176
Clayman, Lieutenant-Colonel 73, 76, 93, 105, 124, 126, 144, 145
Collins, Major-General

Joseph 6, 9, 14, 18, 19, 22, 67, 51, 55, 63, 66, 67, 104, 110, 119, 120, 136, 148, 160, 161, 162, 163-165, 189
Cookson, Lieutenant 172
Dooley, Lieutenant 48, 84
Dulin, Lieutenant-Colonel Thaddeus R 37, 87-88
Eddy, Major-General Manton S 19, 22, 25, 27, 39, 40, 41, 47, 53, 56, 57, 68, 69, 71, 76, 89, 92, 93, 94, 106, 107, 108, 120, 126, 145, 147, 148, 152, 158, 170, 173, 174, 188
Fleming, Commander Ian; RNVR 148
Flint, Colonel Harry 27, 55, 90, 94, 104, 107, 108, 125, 126, 147
Foster, Colonel Robert T 47, 167
Gunn, Lieutenant-Colonel Frank L 55, 125, 126, 147, 152,
Hall, Admiral 66
Hedges, Captain 30
Huff, Lieutenant-Colonel 32, 111, 129, 131, 152, 155, 158
Hurst, Sergeant 157, 186
Jackson, Lieutenant-Colonel Charles L 35, 37, 161
Johnson, Major 116, 134, 135, 136, 139, 141, 161-163
Kauffman, Lieutenant-Colonel Michael B 39, 55, 70, 71, 90, 106
Kelly, Corporal John D 131, 186
Kirby, Lieutenant 155
Koch, Major 97
Kulp, Lieutenant John A 33, 36, 83-86, 179
Landrum, Major-General Eugene M 15
Linder, Captain 88, 99-102, 180
Luckett, Colonel James S 35, 37, 62, 87, 88, 99, 101, 102, 117, 134, 137, 180, 181
Mackelvie, Brigadier-General Jay W 15
MacNeely, Lieutenant-

Colonel Carlton O 35, 36, 60, 61, 83, 86, 112, 113, 179
McCabe, Captain John 95, 96
McCardell Lee 49, 153
McConnell, Major 94, 95
McMahon, Colonel Bernard B 158
Merrill, Lieutenant-Colonel John W 117, 118
Middleton, Major-General Troy H 22
Mitchell, Lieutenant-Colonel Clair B 29, 43, 79
Monk, Lieutenant 57-59
Nutting, Flight Lieutenant David; RAF 45
Ogden, Lieutenant Carlos C 132, 186
Quesada, Major-General Elwood R 67
Rebarchek, Lieutenant John C 34, 36, 112, 113
Ridgway, General Matthew 11, 14
Robinson, Colonel Warren A 32, 43, 45, 81, 97, 110, 129, 132, 155, 157, 184
Rohan, Colonel Frederick J de 19, 26, 39, 40, 41, 53, 55, 68, 69, 70-72, 91-93, 106, 122, 170, 172
Roosevelt, General 137
Simmons, Lieutenant-Colonel Conrad C 33, 36, 82, 98
Smythe, Colonel George W 19, 26, 40, 41, 56, 57, 68, 73, 74, 76, 94, 108, 126, 143, 145, 158-160, 170-173, 187, 189
Sprindus, Captain 172
Strickland, Lieutenant-Colonel Erasmus H 48, 60, 82, 83, 98, 99
Stumpf, Lieutenant-Colonel 55, 104, 125, 174
Teague, Colonel 169
Thorne, Captain Glenn W 163
Tribolet, Colonel 62, 63
Tucker, Lieutenant-Colonel 21, 90
Van Fleet, Colonel James A

191

35-37, 47, 57, 60, 82, 86, 111, 116, 179
Welch, Major 68
Wiggins, Colonel Porter B 31
Williams, Lieutenant 85
Wood, Colonel Stirling A 29, 31, 42, 43, 76, 79, 80, 94, 97, 110, 127, 133
Wyche, Major-General Ira T 22, 28, 31, 32, 33, 42, 46, 59, 76, 80, 81, 95, 97, 108, 110, 133, 138, 152, 153, 155, 157, 183, 185

German Personnel
Dollmann, General Friedrich 175
Graefe, Major 144
Hennecke, Admiral 147
Kauppers, Major 169
Keil, *Oberstleutnant* Guenther 50, 53, 54, 56, 69, 73, 76, 90, 92, 170, 174, 188
Koehn, *Oberst* Walter 50, 57, 59, 76, 79, 81, 82, 178
Mueller, Oberstleutnant Franz 50, 53, 121, 170
Rohrbach, *Oberst* Helmuth 51, 62, 100, 101, 102
Rundstedt, General Gerd von 175
Sattler, *Generalmajor* Robert 103, 145, 158, 189
Schlieben, *Generalleutnant* Karl-Wilhelm von 32, 49-50, 57, 82, 103, 104, 120, 145, 147, 148, 152, 158, 175
Stegmann, *Generalmajor* Rudolf 27

American Formations
First Army 22, 66
V Corps 9, 14, 15
VII Corps 6, 9, 11, 14, 22, 33, 47, 49, 51, 55, 59, 66, 68, 103, 120, 121, 136, 141, 161, 165, 175, 183
VIII Corps 18, 22, 176

Air Force
IX Tactical Air Command 67
Armoured 70th Tank Battalion 37, 83, 97, 98, 113, 118
746th Tank Battalion 106

Artillery
29th Field Artillery Battalion 112
44th Field Artillery Battalion 167, 169
60th Field Artillery Battalion 21

Engineers
4th Engineer Combat Battalion 23

Infantry
4th Division 12, 13, 23, 33-38, 46-48, 59-64, 82-88 97-102, 111-118, 134-142, 167, 176, 178-182
8th Regiment 33-35, 46, 48, 59, 82, 97, 111, 115, 134, 179
12th Regiment 33, 35-37, 46, 86-88, 99, 100, 111, 116, 118, 134, 136, 138, 161, 162, 167, 180, 181
22nd Regiment 37, 38, 48, 62-64, 117, 134
9th Division 14, 18, 19-22, 25-28, 39-41, 50, 53-57, 66, 68, 69-76, 89-94, 104-108, 120, 121-127, 143-152, 158-160, 170, 186-189
39th Regiment 20, 25-27, 41, 53, 55, 76, 90, 94, 104, 106-108, 125-127, 145, 147-148, 174
47th Regiment 19, 27, 40, 41, 56, 57, 68, 73, 76, 90, 93, 104, 106-108, 122, 126, 143, 158, 170-172, 187, 188, 189
60th Regiment 19-22, 25, 27, 39-41, 53, 68, 69, 71, 72, 76, 90-93, 106-108, 121, 169, 170, 173, 188
79th Division 22, 25-27, 28-33, 42-46, 50, 57-59, 66, 76-82, 94-97, 108-111, 127-133, 152-158, 176, 178, 182-186
313th Regiment 29, 31, 33, 42, 43, 46, 57, 76, 79, 81, 94, 95, 97, 110, 111, 127, 129, 133, 152, 155, 183-186
314th Regiment 31, 42, 43, 46, 76, 80, 81, 96-97 109-111, 129, 132, 153, 155, 183,

184-186
315th Regiment 31, 42, 76, 80, 81, 158, 183, 184
82nd Airborne Division 13, 18, 19
505th Regiment 11
507th Regiment 11
508th Regiment 11
90th Division 15, 18, 27
359th Infantry Regiment 27
101st Airborne Division 11, 12, 13-15, 44, 176
501st Regiment 11
505th Regiment 11
507th Regiment 11
Reconnaissance 4th Cavalry Group 25, 27, 29, 38, 53, 55
24th Cavalry Squadron 38
79th Reconnaissance Troop 29

British Formation
30 Assault Unit, Royal Marines 45, 148

German Formations
Seventh Army 9, 20, 52, 57, 103, 175
243rd Division 50
Kampfgruppen Mueller 50, 53, 121
Kampfgruppen Keil 53, 54, 56, 69, 73, 76, 90
Kampfgruppen Koehn 50, 57, 59, 76, 79, 81, 82, 94, 111, 118, 178
Kampfgruppen Rohrbach 62, 101
729th Regiment 50
739th Regiment 50
919th Regiment 50, 170
921st Regiment 24
922nd Regiment 170
17th Machine Gun Battalion 50
Sturm Battalion AOK 7 24
30th Flak Regiment 73
310th Marine Boat Fleet 57
Organisation Todt 49, 110

Others
French underground 28, 57, 90, 125, 161
V1 Rockets 44-45, 82, 99, 179